CONFESSIONS OF A TANTRIC LAWYER

A Unique Guide to Magnetise Your Magical Life

By Kim Mukti Nirjhara

First published in 2023 by Kim, Mukti Nirjhara

© Kim, Mukti Nirjhara

The moral rights of the author have been asserted.
This book is an Inspirational Book Writers book.

Author: Nirjhara, Kim Mukti
Title: Confessions of a Tantric Lawyer; A Unique Guide to Magnetise Your Magical Life
ISBN: 9798867816070

Editor-in-chief: Keziah Daniel
Cover Design: Sarah Rose Graphic Design

Disclaimer:
The material in this publication is of the nature of general professional advice, but it is not intended to provide specific guidance for particular circumstances and it should not be relied on as the basis for any decision to take action or not take action on any particular matter which it covers. Readers should obtain individual advice from the author where appropriate, before making any such decision. To the maximum extent permitted by law, the author and publisher disclaim all responsibility and liability to any person, arising directly or indirectly from any person taking or not taking action based on the information in this publication.

*"The greatest fear in the world is the opinion of others,
and the moment you are unafraid of the crowd, you are no
longer a sheep, you become a lion.
A great roar arises in your heart, the roar of freedom.
…Creativity is the greatest rebellion in existence…."*
– Osho

*"Take your well-disciplined strengths and stretch them
between two opposing poles. Because inside human beings
is where God learns."*
– Rilke via Bruce Lyon

What People Say

Robin's Powerful Decision To Change Her Life

'My sessions with Kim were critical to opening up my heart and soul to joy that I never thought was meant for me.

She took my hand (metaphorically speaking) and guided me though a veritable art gallery of beautiful possibilities that were mine for the choosing.

Until I allowed Kim on my life journey, I was following a path that was created from 'smoke and mirrors'…a path based on antiquated cultural lore and the banalities of societal dogma.

 I am grateful to God for giving me the courage to sign on to sessions with Kim.

I am now reaping the benefits of a life of love and joy that I truly believe is meant for us all!'
- Robin T, ridiculously happy spouse, mother and musician
wwwrobintreybig.com

Annie Overcame Blocks To a Successful Compensation Claim

'In 2018, USA Gymnastics (USAG) convicted its Head Olympic Coach of assaulting young girls and women for 20+ years.

This conviction sparked deep research into other complaints for every gym registered with USAG.

Hundreds of stories were hushed and wiped under the rug. Mine was one of those stories.

After 20 years of nobody listening to me, I got a letter in the mail, requesting a conversation about a complaint that I filed in the early 90s as a child.

There was a great relief of finally having my story validated, but a huge distrust in myself that it created... As well as the system.

I had multiple attorneys reaching out to me to see if I wanted to be a part of the litigation and financial benefit from the victims claim fund.

Most of them were cold and unfeeling focused on results and completion of this form... and I'm sure their own financial compensation as well.

I held onto the form for a year before I could bring myself to write my story.

I learned about Kim a few years previous in healing communities.

Despite being in an entirely different country, I knew Kim's passion for healing in a language that I understood, and my body understood...

A depth of knowledge of legal transactions and forms made Kim the best person to help me open the door on a story that for years no one believed.

She helped me open to tell a story that was overwhelming, invited a calmness throughout my body so I could recall the event more completely - it happened 20 years ago!

Kim aided peace and breath back to my body. She was able to weave the energetics of healing into words that fit the legal form for the USA attorneys to take forward and helped with emotional clearing for me to stand more solidly for adjudication.

Thank-you so much!'

- Annie D, wife, mother and business owner

Steve Avoided Litigation And Peacefully Resolved A Contract Dispute

'I'm a Permaculture teacher, landscape gardener, designer and builder of eco-villages in Australia.

It took everything I had and more to finish construction of the Aldinga Arts Eco-Village, one of the largest legal intentional community developments in the world.

Sadly, one of my then fellow eco-village company directors got ill with cancer, with devastating results.

Accounts were unpaid, creditors threatened to sue.

At this time, I'd invested all I had for over a decade by way of my time and personal funds, designed and built the landscape, co-written the Village By-Laws etc, sat for hours in various government bureaucrats' offices, to work through the red tape.

I got to know Kim when I was at the end of my tether, had chronic neck pain, was not able to work, found it difficult to work, litigation was threatened.

Unwell and depressed, I thought it seemed we had no choice but to go to court.

I invited Kim to help sort out the mess that was my life. She referred me to a physiotherapist who understands the mind body connection and I started using a posture pole, which relieved the neck pain.

Kim systematically went through the eco-village company emails, concluded that there was no point in litigation, the situation required mediation, and she knew the right person.

Mediation was cathartic - just being in the one room together.

At one point one person left and we thought all was lost, but they returned.

We ended the day with hugs, tears and a peaceful resolution!

I was finally able to move on, sell my block in the Village, follow my dreams to outback tour guide, taking people to spectacular sacred sites and working with Aboriginal Elders.

I'm so grateful for Kim's assistance in one of the darkest times of my life with her healing and legal experience.

The Arts Eco-Village is thriving, its success has attracted much attention as a way for how humans can thrive in harmony with nature and each other.'
- Stephen Poole, https://stephenpoolepermaculture.com

Interview with Kerry, Increased His Income, High End Clients, Leadership Skills, Started Holding Community Events

Q: What was your life like before working with me for 3 months?

A: I had a lot of ideas about what I'd like but was having trouble making things happen, I didn't have the tools to move into a grounded place.

Q: Did you have many doubts or obstacles to overcome?

A: Many internal obstacles, resistance to timelines, expectations, deadlines which I needed to shift. I didn't think online sessions would work, yet found them great, very interesting. I learned to trust the process. I always dreamed of doing more fulfilling things but lacked courage.

Since working with you I've had more high-end clients. I've organised many events, twice run a successful three-day self-development residential retreat. It's become a regular event at an independent resort with many facilitators. People came from interstate, had a ball and are still talking about it. I started doing self-clearing, now I have more awareness of kinesiology testing.

Q: Wow amazing. What made you the happiest about our sessions?

A: The leaning into the mystery part, my rational brain still doesn't completely accept it, the Computer Programmer in me is sceptical – yet I've seen all the stuff from the past shifting. The biggest change is in finding the power of expression, I'm clearer, purposeful & truthful. I even had work meetings where I was able to speak from my heart about what I could achieve. I stepped up in what I could offer.

My income increased a lot. Working with you helped me to open up and allow this to happen

Q: What would you suggest to someone who is thinking of working with me?

A: Don't over-think it. Trust in the mystery and the possibility of opening up. It's a bit like having a chiropractic treatment...I'm not sure why it works but it feels much better! THANK-YOU!

- Kerry, IT Consultant and Father of Three

Interview with Jacquie: From Guilt And Chronic Indecision To Power Freedom Awareness, And A Dream Holiday Overseas

Q: What was it like before we did 9 sessions over 3 months?

A: Before I felt really lost, overwhelmed by everything: work, family life, finances.

I was utterly stuck. Every time I tried to make decisions I ended up falling in a heap. I needed help getting out of that dark, stuck place. I realised I was holding onto a lot of guilt which was holding me back from my true potential. With your support, bit by bit I let go of that stuff.

Now there's a light at the end of the tunnel. My thought patterns are so different. I feel stronger and in control of what I do. I'm much more certain of my decisions, that I'm making the right ones, and I don't feel bad about my decisions anymore.

Q: What were the problems you were trying to solve?

A: I was always so concerned about what my family would think of me and felt overly responsible for others. Now it's very exciting, I've let go of guilt, without forcing anything or being harsh. I can speak truth without feeling controlled by others, and they have come around more, my connections are closer.

Q: Where did you start your search for help?

A: I had a stack of second-hand magazines on "Life and health", I read an article and it was all about energy, I became interested. I always knew there was more to life than what I experienced, that it was possible to feel more, closer emotional bonds and sacredness.

Q: What made my work stand out?

A: I read your website, was very intrigued, it really resonated with me. I longed to throw myself into something that had immediate effects. At the end of our sessions, I always felt a billion percent more positive. I felt so good and that I was heading in the right direction.

My attitude has completely changed, it's exceeded my expectations.

I started to notice changes really quickly, it still blows me away.

I have more contentment in what I do and say, also more confidence, I don't doubt myself as I have ability to feel confident to speak when I need to, I no longer have feelings of guilt and I don't worry about the result.

It really surprised me how quickly it worked, how thorough it was, and how comfortable I was talking about things.

I couldn't wait for our sessions each fortnight, there were times I got emotional, but it was all extremely beneficial.

After we finished our sessions, I finally took my dream holiday overseas, and had the experiences of a lifetime I will treasure forever, connecting with family in the UK.

I thoroughly recommend your work for people seeking the truth who really want to understand themselves, to get to the bottom of it all. Working with Kim will set you in the right direction.'

- Jacquie

Chris Released Emotional Blocks

'After working together I felt more relaxed I'd ever felt in my life, it was amazing. A lot of pressure and tension released. I released emotional blocks I was holding onto since childhood. Thank-you for a wonderful experience you have a healing heart!'

- Chris, Personal Fitness Trainer

More Client Testimonials

'Since our sessions I am feeling relieved of guilt. I realised that I have been acting to please people to get acknowledged and validation. No more about this! I have shed this need. I realized I have to take care of ME...in all aspects of my life and I am allowed to be the first important person! Boundaries are clearer. Thank you for your time.'

- Colette, Nurse

'After our sessions I am optimistic for the future. It does feel like a great burden has lifted off my shoulders. Thank you for your help and care.'

- Mark, Farmer, South Australia

'I came to see you because I have had cysts removed from my ovaries and I want to work with clearing blockages, so they don't return. Now after several sessions my body is much healthier and I am happier, terrific ever since. Thanks heaps, see you again soon.'

- Sue, Business Manager

'After the first session I felt good with more energy. I felt more positive and confident and slept less. On my second session, wow it happened for me. Transformation to achieve my long-term dream of feeling more in control of my sexual and emotional energy and happy in my life! Thanks for the information and for being a wonderful teacher :)'

- Peter, Intellectual Property Lawyer

'I'm doing much better. I'm more balanced after suffering a nervous disorder, thanks.'

- Nelly, Disability Support Worker

'Thanks for the session, yes I have noticed some changes, my mind and body is more connected. I have also had two things manifest within 24 hours after the last session which was amazing!'

- Shane, Machinist

'It was very good working with you, I've more positive thoughts and energy. Thanks again and it was a terrific experience.'

- Abdul, Engineer

'I felt very peaceful and clear after the sessions. I'm doing more meditation which also helped to shift things.'

- Carol, Scientist

'I had a flood of emotions since the session. It has brought up some suppressed emotions, though I also enjoyed the work, it felt lovely.'

- Suzy, Researcher, Adelaide

'I enjoyed our session. Time went very fast. In the past I've suffered from panic attacks and avoided certain situations. Lately I've been meditating which has helped. I'm more able to contemplate taking more challenging steps towards my growth.'

- Erica, Electrician, Sydney

'I felt very safe coming in for my session with Kim. I didn't know what to expect but from our discussions it felt right. I am amazed by her level of experience so knew I was in safe hands. I learnt some valuable tools from Kim and since the session I have felt many things shift for me. I also feel that I have made a beautiful friend which is such a blessing.'

- Kristen, videographer/digital marketer

'After working with you on my relationship issues it's incredible! Instead of thinking there's something wrong with me, I've finally accepted that I can't fulfil all my partner's needs. This is an opportunity I didn't think I'd have. Thanks, the sessions helped me feel a thousand times better!' ☺

- Claudia, Artist

'After my session I now feel more empowered and confident. I look forward to continuing the journey in future.'

- Dave, Financial Consultant

'Our work helped me get more equilibrium and inspiration. I'm more expressive and talk about my feelings, ideas and thoughts. I've regained focus, motivation and passion back into my life. I know I have much to offer society/humanity. Thanks so much!'

- Terry, Town Planner

'After working together I'm feeling good, lots more creative sexual energy. I'd love to stay open. I imagine your suggestion of the Jade Egg will be good for that. Thank-you for your time, I'm very grateful.'

- Sunita, Marketing Manager, Sydney

'I am an older gentleman who saw you for help with A SERIOUS MEDICAL ISSUE, (I refuse to take the pills etc)

WOW like a weight has lifted from my body. I am ready to conquer anything. it's amazing!'

- Harry, Naturopath/Acupuncturist

What People Say About Soul Journey Akashic Records Readings With Kim

'Hi I'm Debs and I have such gratitude for having Kim as a trusted advisor in my world. Thanks to her guidance in the past two years, I have true and accurate information. After all my sessions with Kim I leave with my soul at ease and my spirit ignited. Inner guidance has been clarified. Kim's miracles of insight and advice have transformed my personal and professional life. Without hesitancy I would recommend Kim.'

- Debs, Social Innovator

'I had an Akashic Record reading with Kim and my experience was lovely! The reading felt like a deep conversion with a dear and wise friend. Kim was able to share information in a clear and friendly way, with full presence and heart. At the end of the session I felt more clarity about personal issues as well as a feeling of ease and lightness. A short time after our session I ended up meeting the man of my dreams. We now have a beautiful little girl. I recommend Kim very much.'

- Gloria, Film-maker, UK

What People Say About This Book

'In a linear world, Confessions of a Tantric Lawyer introduces the circle...The place where extremities meet and everything else can be held. Vibrant and full of life, it's a page turner that welcomes us into the author's fearlessly lived life whilst encouraging the reader to embrace the many aspects of ourselves.'

- Avanti Shivpuri, International Healer,
(http://avantishivpuri.com)

'Confessions of a Tantric Lawyer weaves a magical bridge between the left brain (Law) and the right brain (Tantra).'

We all view the world through our own eyes, and to me this book is to law like what Dr Joe Dispenza is to manifesting healing…a bridge between science and the mystical - law on the one hand which is three dimensional and tantra, spirituality on the other, which are multi-dimensional.

There are so many gold nuggets in this book and Kim is absolutely right, if we can introduce more spiritual practices into our schools, we would definitely see happier adults and as a result happier children and a happier, healthier world in general. When children are taught the sacredness of our human bodies, so much of life is different, it becomes more awe-inspiring and harmonious.

As an Intuitive coach and healer, I see people daily who are working through some form of trauma. When I teach the basics of awareness, and help them come into alignment, I see a massive change almost instantly. All these basic skills can be taught and done by children and adults alike. They just need to be made aware of it and this book certainly brings the two worlds closer together."

- Leonie Du Toit: The Awareness Mentor, Intuitive Coach, Healer, Author (www.leoniedutoit.com)

'Tantra is an often misunderstood and distorted concept. Kim's stories of her delicious adventures on roads less travelled relate how the sacred wisdom of Tao & Osho interconnects and aligns to the natural laws of First Nations across time and continents from the Celtic druids through the Inca lands and Australian Aboriginal and Torres Strait Islander People.'

- Justin Lodge, Author of three Amazon #1 bestselling books, including 'Making Darkness Visible', (https:/justinlodge. substack.com)

'Kim's book is a profound remarkable heart-warming and fearless true story of her journey to live a meaningful life of truth. Exploring the many themes of love, freedom, and nature her words of compassion and wisdom are profound and revered. She has created and danced the mysteries of her own path of imagination and dreams. She has found the freedom to find the gifts of her own teaching of moral law within herself. Facing her challenges and overcoming the burdens of life, each chapter finds the refuge in humanity.

The book triumphs when Kim finds and cultivates a place in her soul where there is great love warmth and forgiveness to reach her own healing. Not in isolation but in community. She's an inspiration and a champion of beliefs and self-healing. Moving through the storm and weeping into her dance, she has unified us and inspired us to reach for stars hidden in the landscapes of our souls. To find our own sunset to reach our inner peace of stillness.'

- Suzie Craddock Accredited 5 rhythms teacher Perth Western Australia

'A Blueprint for a New Way of Life.'

It's no secret that we are moving into unprecedented times. What used to work, has either already broken, or is showing signs of serious decay. Humanity is re-imagining itself. People everywhere are looking for new ways to live, work and play.

I believe that Kim's new book is a blueprint for a new way of life. One that marries the practical with the spiritual. One that considers and embodies true humanity. It's a book that gives its readers permission to fully be themselves, in all their ways - even if society would say "hold on, you can't be that AND that".

You might not be a lawyer. You might not be into tantra. But the lessons inside this book will awaken you to new possibilities for living a magical life, whatever that looks like for you.'

- Dave Thompson, founder, Inspirational Book Writers

The Phoenix – a symbol of rebirth, renewal and hope
Original Art by Drew Straker

Dedication

This book is dedicated to my Soul Tribe: partners, lovers, friends, family, teachers, colleagues, clients – you're a constant inspiration and reminder of who I truly am.

To my darling, feisty, trail-blazing mother and best friend, there is no greater gift than life itself.

To Dad, my stepdad, wonderful grandparents, you're always in my heart.

To all of you bright lights, I am eternally grateful for your shining.

Foreword

This book is a guide for adventurous souls looking to expand their life, explore their unique soul journey, and step into their personal power. A useful tool illustrating a fast track for personal development no matter who you identify as or where you are on the spiritual path – as a beginner developing interest in these topics, or an advanced spiritual practitioner.

Most compelling is Kim's ability to draw parallels between the principles of law and Tantra. Through skilful storytelling, she highlights how the pursuit of justice in the legal realm and the quest for spiritual enlightenment in Tantra both require empathy, a holistic perspective, and a deep understanding of human nature.

With a playful, whimsical style, the emotions expressed are both palpable and tangible. The extraordinary bravery of the author in sharing these deeply personal experiences, professional consequences be damned, shows what a powerhouse this woman is, and is deeply inspiring for anyone concerned about how others may view them. Kim is a truly devoted spiritual renegade, her inimitable journey encapsulates her profound insights, the pages seem infused with the essence of mysticism and introspection.

The narrative is a blend of soul searching, legal anecdotes, and insights into Tantra, making it an absorbing read for both legal professionals and those interested in spirituality. Readers are likely to come away from this book with a newfound appreciation for the depths of human experience and the potential for growth in unexpected places.

This remarkable work of introspection and revelation embodies the convergence of two worlds: western law, which is deeply rooted within the materialistic worldview, and Tantra, a powerful path of personal transformation.

What sets this work apart is not only the wealth of experience Kim brings but also the depth of her reflection. The pages pulse with authenticity as she divulges her deeply personal experiences and revelations, and it is a joy to read. As you hear about the intricate cases and the solemn chambers of justice, you'll also explore the sacred spaces of meditation and the transformative energy of Tantra. This book transcends mere narrative; it's an invitation to partake in a voyage of self-discovery and understanding, weaving individual threads which liberate new colour and texture to the fabric of our human lives.

As you immerse yourself in these pages, I encourage you to embrace the profound lessons that lie therein. My greatest wish is that this book may kindle your inner fire of inquiry. May it inspire you to embrace the synergies of your own unique journey – to see the beauty in the convergence of seemingly disparate worlds, and to embrace the transformation that comes from that union.

Kim has created more than a book; she has crafted an open invitation to explore the unchartered territories of your own life.

May this journey reading Confessions of a Tantric Lawyer be transformative, one that unlocks hidden potentials and unravels the mysteries that reside within.

Sarah Phoenixfire – Cornerstone Academy

Preface

Confessions of a Tantric Lawyer is an inspirational and amazing memoir in which Kim breaks down the old stories of what it is to be a woman and indeed a human, sharing her dynamic, fully conscious life choices. Her stories of a free and cageless journey of joy and self-expression open gateways some may never have imagined possible.

The mainstream medical lens for viewing human experience has us creating separation and "otherness" for those whose states of reality are outside our scope of understanding, through discounting a holistic picture of an individual operating on multiple planes. The result is that within the community, we are at a loss when it comes to supporting friends, loved ones, colleagues, and family members with such experiences beyond the scope of our own knowledge and understanding. Additionally, rather than making a peripheral assessment of an individual during a point of crisis, they should be seen and understood within the context of their life experience, self-held stories and beliefs, cultural, religious, and ancestral background. The medical system might surmise that patterns within families are due to the genetic nature of mental illness, but intergenerational trauma is also now proven to be carried at a cellular level.

Many of us have an awareness of the significance and even reverence afforded to experiences of "altered states" within other (non-western) cultures. Western society is unable to integrate this dichotomy, allowing our medical system to solely dominate and control the social position and responses to these states. We are so profoundly lost with only a two-dimensional western medical model to hold us and those who seek to link us with support. In this way, spiritual emergence – the whispering of the soul's messages to light our next steps forward – becomes spiritual emergency. Exploring the spiritual meanings and wisdom underpinning altered state experiences and life's crises is like finding missing puzzle pieces, long-lost friends, and being set free from the negative connotations of the medical model.

Seen through a spiritual, holistic lens, the world is not one of disorder, illness, or dysfunction but one of resilience, strength, and resurrection. Without a language for what is happening to us and without those equipped to interpret, guide, hold, reassure, listen, and debrief with, life becomes a cataclysm of humanity. Like the phoenix rising from the ashes, crises and altered states can act as keystones for life transitions, wake-up calls, and calls to healing where messages are received, reflected, and integrated. With each comes the opportunity for deep introspection and review of *"who I am and where I've come from"*. Often, they lead to major life changes or different approaches based on new insights and realisations that arose during the altered state and its integration.

This book is utterly engaging reading. It illustrates that what's missing is the ancient and wise practice of mentorship, a spiritual guide or space holder in these landscapes of "health" and "wellbeing".

Kate McIntyre – Social Worker specialising in Intergenerational Trauma work
(lighthousetherapy.my.canva.site; Lighthouse Therapy on Sacred Earth (FB)

Introduction

Who this book is for and who it's not for:

This book is for Spiritual Seekers, Curious Creatives, Old Souls, Wounded Healers, Adventurous Spirits, Questing Queens, Lost Knights, Weird Witches, and basically anyone who feels they don't 'fit in' or just wonders, 'is life more than it seems?'

This book is NOT for anyone who loves following rules and hates moving out of their comfort zone.

If that's you, **PUT THE BOOK DOWN NOW!**

I SAID, PUT IT DOWN!

Unless of course you are a secret rebel or ninja at heart.

What is a Tantric Lawyer, anyway?

A Tantric Lawyer is a rare creature, a hybrid of opposites of sorts.

To many people, Tantra invokes unusual sexual positions, like as pictured in the Kama Sutra, which look both incredible and impossible! ☺

Tantra is fast-track personal development. Rocket fuel for the Soul.

Tantra sees everything in life as sensations, which our mind attaches judgement to – right, wrong, desirable and undesirable.

Tantra can be used to heal from broken relationships, broken bodies, minds, and broken bank accounts. Tantra is mind over matter and mind in matter.

Tantra includes sexuality, it's potent life force energy, which is highly repressed and contained in Western culture. As I am writing this, a number of sexual assault and harassment allegations in Parliament are taking up time in the news, revenge porn crime has doubled in the past two years… Tantra has never been more needed in the mainstream.

So what is Tantra? Tantra weaves opposite polarities together, such as:

Mind and body
Sex and heart
Expansion and contraction
Emotions and detachment
Soul and personality
Male and female
Hard and soft
Yin and yang
Cold and hot
Spirit and matter
Earth and the Black Hole at the centre of the galaxy

Tantric or kundalini energy is our life-force, also called prana or chi. It's common for difficult emotions like anger, sadness, shame, and guilt to get stuck in our body, especially around our heart and sexuality. When these emotions are felt, expressed, and cleared, we feel more alive, connected to cosmic or universal energy, the most powerful force in the world.

Tantra is a path of transformation through the body. Taoist Tantra focuses on longevity, health, and wellbeing. Pure Tantra is more interested in consciousness. Tao means the Way, Spiritual, Universal Law, the natural order of the Universe. Chi is the energy guiding everything in the Universe.

So how does Tantra fit with being a Lawyer, I hear you ask?

People often say,

it's hard to imagine a person who does both…

I've been a Lawyer for over thirty years, and a Tantrika for over twenty, and I think that LAW NEEDS MORE TANTRA, AND TANTRA NEEDS MORE LAW.

Western law is based on the mind, a materialistic paradigm. This has served us in getting to where we are, but it's not holistic, the cracks are starting to show. More and more people feel anxious; even though we live more comfortably and with fewer threats than ever before, so-called 'wicked problems' are increasing.

To explain further, I have two jokes.

First, did you hear the one about the person who asked seven lawyers the answer to one plus one?

1. The family lawyer said it's a marriage – but first you need a prenuptial agreement, and later you may need a divorce and child custody and property settlements.
2. The business lawyer said it's a partnership — you'll need a watertight agreement, and a lawyer if it's dissolved.
3. The criminal lawyer said it means joint and several liability, you'll need two lawyers.
4. The estate lawyer said you can get a discount from joint wills for a couple and probate applications after death.

5. The intellectual property lawyer said one invention plus one patent equals money!
6. The corporate lawyer said a company director and secretary equals a company, freedom to conduct business all over the world.
7. The sole legal practitioner says, hmmm one plus one…
    closes the blinds, curtains, and
    whispers
    very softly… *WHAT DO YOU WANT THE ANSWER TO BE?*

So, you get the idea that everything depends on your perspective. One of the first things they teach you at law school is that truth and law are completely separate.

I see law as a cultural narrative; it used to mean 'manner' or 'custom' and has strayed a long way from Spiritual, Universal, or Natural Law, which is a body of unchanging moral, ethical principles.

Law is actually very creative – Amazing Grace, 18th Century England

The true story behind the song Amazing Grace, which I really love, is about a sea captain of a slave ship who got caught in the worst storm he'd ever encountered, with a boat full of African slaves. The captain really thought it was the end and that his ship would go down with all the people on board. For the first time in his life, he started to pray.

He said, "God I've never believed in you or spoken to you before. You have no reason to listen to me now. I've lived a rough, selfish life, my sole existence has been to profit from my slave trade. I'm a hard man, and I never paid you a second thought. If you do exist, these are my last moments. I can't see my boat surviving this storm. If we make it safely to shore, I promise to become a better man and turn over a new leaf. Please, please, I'm begging you, please deliver us from this storm."

The sea captain was interrupted from his last rite prayers by an unearthly, beautiful sound of singing. The African slaves were singing to the waves, and unbelievably, the waves were calming down!

The boat made it to shore, and the sea captain, true to his word, went on to set all the slaves free. He even gave statements as evidence about the conditions of the slave boats to the anti-slave campaigners who petitioned to William Wilberforce in the late 18th century.

The 2006 film, 'Amazing Grace', recounts the story of how it wasn't just numerous petitions, but it took some creative imagination and theatrics to end slavery for good.

I think law needs re-visioning, our world is changing faster than ever before in recorded history.

So what qualifies me to talk about law and spiritual law? This is my story, based on my experience. It's raw and deeply personal.

I've been a general legal practitioner for over thirty years… in ALL areas of law, in three Australian States, and in London in the UK.

I've been a PhD law candidate at a top-tier University – proposing a radical duty of care to Earth and its inhabitants for sustainability and harmony, with an Aboriginal case study.

Law is based on precedent, decisions made by others in the past, sometimes hundreds of years ago – it was designed to grow empires and economies, and to keep the peace.

This reminds me of another joke, this one about a child, and children, unlike most adults, are not afraid to tell the truth! The child asked her Dad (it's a modern family) why he cut off the top and bottom of the roast before putting it in the pan to cook.

The Dad said, "I don't know, my mother always used to do that."

The child asked her Grandma, "Grandma, why do you cut the top and bottom off the roast before you cook it?"

Grandma said, "I don't know, my mother used to do that."

The child asked her GREAT-GRANDMOTHER, "Why do you cut the top and bottom off the roast?"

The great-grandmother laughed and said, "Because my oven pan was too small to fit the whole roast!"

The moral of the story is that there was probably a very good reason for doing things a particular way, once upon a time.

If things aren't working, the definition of insanity is to keep doing them the same way and expect a different result.

In my experience, law no longer suits our understanding of ourselves and the world, it was designed a long time ago for a very different world to the one we live in now. The research on so-called wicked problems of modern society connected to law could probably fill a small country, or at least an island!

This book is my journey of how I have woven together law and ancient mystic tantric teachings.

I've also explored First Nations lore, which is based on caring for country, where all life is regarded as sacred and connected, and where the object of law is maintaining harmony and balance.

THE PURPOSE OF THIS BOOK IS TO WAKE YOU UP TO WHO YOU REALLY ARE…

a magician, witch, wizard, creatrix, author, builder, designer, and midwife of a new and much better world. And if you know this, to confirm you're on the right path.

While I hope that everyone reads this book,
it's written for anyone who's looking to expand their life!
You don't have to be a Tantrika or Lawyer to get something
out of this book.

Chapters

Chapter 1

Turning a Wound into a Magical Wand – Manifesting through the Heart

A Tantric Lawyer in Training!

Being a lawyer and tantric healer, I realised that it was hard for me to completely let go; I was always good at fixing other people's problems and holding a healing space – helping others have a better life.

My earliest memory is of wanting people to love each other; I always knew I wanted to help make the world a better place. From a young age, I became very good at tuning into others, and less proficient at tuning into myself. As the eldest child, I played caretaker and emotionally monitored my parents and siblings.

For my first six years I had an ideal early life, plenty of space to roam, a creek at the bottom of our big yard, and was precocious and adored. I was bright and could read novels aloud before I went to school, my first was *'Charlie and the Chocolate Factory'* by Roald Dahl.

I had plenty of playmates, creative expression, love, and outdoor time – everything a child could want or need. I was confident and sexually curious in the innocently erotic way of children. I recall playing games like 'body doctors' with boys my age, telling several boys that I loved them, and promising to marry them! I have joyful memories of houseboat holidays with a group of families doing naked swimming, sunbathing, body painting, and mud sliding.

The book '*Open Marriage*' was published in 1972. My parents and their friends started to explore the new revolutionary consciousness with sweet innocence and naiveté. That was, until through a discussion group, Mum met the man who later became my stepfather. They bonded on communication courses, fell in love, and then… things fell apart.

Open Marriage, Broken Marriage

The summer after my first year of school, my family went to another Australian city for a holiday by plane, which was a huge adventure. At the end of it, my Mum and brother got on the plane and returned home. I remained in a tiny flat with Dad and our cat Smokey. This was amazing, for Dad had never kept house or parented on his own, except for short periods of time. And it is a testimony to his strength of character and love that he chose to care for a young daughter at a time when it was unheard of for fathers to be sole parents.

At the age of 6, I went into caretaking mode towards Dad, tried my best to be cheerful and entertaining, preparing snacks from my Pooh Bear cookbook, sometimes burning the food and my fingers as I learnt.

To cope with the new situation – my losses, my life felt scary – I developed some strange behaviours, which helped me to feel more in control. I sometimes counted to 20 before going to the toilet or even before riding my bike down a hill with my eyes shut. These things gave me permission to feel pain. If I totalled my bike and had scrapes on my body, the crashes gave me an excuse to cry and be comforted.

Psychologists now know that deliberate self-harm is a way (albeit an ultimately unhelpful way) to express and manage emotions such as anxiety, sadness, shame, and anger, providing a temporary escape from emotional pain. Although it can bring a kind of temporary relief from painful emotions, they do return and intensify later, not to mention the risk of hurting oneself badly.

As a child and young adult, I often struggled with health issues, numerous colds and flus, which I believe was due to repressed feelings about the family separation. It was more than just the separation I was adjusting to; it was also the big changes I saw in my parents, and the loss of my own childhood and innocence. As I grew up fast, I repressed my challenging feelings and needs, took comfort in my books, became a model student, and excelled at school.

There was genuinely pure, extremely strong emotion involved in the marital separation, and then there was what the court process did to my parents. Everything became weaponised. Mutual friends and family were asked to write affidavits (sworn statements) to the Court of what a good parent one was and how bad the other was. Unfortunately, this dysfunctional relationship continued until I grew up.

Change is Never All Bad

For the two-and-a-half years I lived with Dad, I enjoyed an extraordinary amount of freedom. I ate only food kids love and watched anything I wanted on TV. I made a friend who had ponies and another who had baby chicks at home – her parents taught me to eat properly with a knife and fork – I was thrilled to meet the animals.

There was one babysitter I was particularly fond of and saw regularly. Katie, a drama student. She told the truth and funny stories. One night we played balloon tennis so energetically, the downstairs neighbour complained – Katie said she should have pretended to only speak a foreign language. She was a hoot.

A Child of the Sexual Revolution

I grew up in the seventies, the era of liberation. Women were burning their bras. Sexuality was out of the closet. I read my Dad's *'Mad and Penthouse'* magazines and an imaginative book of pornographic fairy tales, transfixed by colourfully illustrated stories of Prince Charming's lingam bursting out of his trousers when he saw Cinderella in her ball-gown, and the Giantess inserting Jack and his beans into her giant yoni.[1]

From a young age I innocently self-pleasured using a teddy bear, then later a pillow, and readily fell in love with male icons on TV. In this environment my natural currents of energy flowed. Since then, in my breathwork and other meditation processes, I have had many 'past life memories' or visions of working in sacred sexuality temples. As a child I would also imagine being a shackled sex worker, which is a common female fantasy (hence the popularity of the *'Fifty Shades of Grey'* series about a sexually dominating lead male character, which sold millions).

As much as it gives me great joy to recall these memories, it also saddens me greatly that our sexual life force energy is so misunderstood, distorted, and abused on our planet. As I write this, domestic violence incidents dominate the media, and law enforcement struggles to contain the enforced prostitution and sex trafficking of mostly women and children, which goes on.

---

[1] 'Lingam' means 'wand of light, healing tool' and 'Yoni' means 'sacred space' in Sanskrit, Tantric words for male and female genitals

Even in our so-called advanced post-industrial society, violence is endemic; police and courts cannot cope.[2]

The Brady Bunch without an Alice

After what seemed like a protracted and acrimonious family court trial, I moved back to live with my Mum, brother, stepdad, and stepsisters (who lived with us half the time). From the age of six to eighteen, each school holiday, three or four times per year, I visited the other parent by plane, clocking up thousands of aeroplane miles.

Life was busy in our large, blended family. The next-door neighbour would yell to shut us up when we sang ABBA songs in the backyard, and occasionally he threw walnuts at us, which made us laugh.

As a 'latch-key kid', I spent hours outdoors playing with horses, football, hopscotch, through creeks, and riding our bikes to hills that we climbed and slid down on our bottoms when they were slippery in the winter.

A Taste for Freedom

My stepdad was a charismatic French-speaking Jewish refugee from Egypt, whose family moved to Australia after his elder brother, a doctor, was imprisoned in post-war Cairo. His brother-in-law, Fred, had been in Auschwitz and only survived due to wearing long trousers the day the inmates were separated into boys and adult men. Those who wore shorts were sent to the gas chambers, and those who wore long trousers were deemed old

---

[2] There is vast literature on law's role in creating a 'dominator culture'. The most influential on me was '*The Chalice and the Blade*' by Riane Eisler, a lawyer who advocates that sacred sexuality can play a healing role in ending violence.

enough to work. That day saved Fred's life, he was able to work in the horse stables. The horses ate better than the inmates, but Fred was able to steal enough horse food to survive.

My siblings and I were all bright and cheeky, we were encouraged particularly by my stepdad to question everything – rules, trends, and fashions. He was witty and observant, and when we wanted to do what other children did, seeing the toxicity of a culture which encouraged girls from a young age to be overly concerned about their appearance, he had sayings like 'why be a lemming?'

Early Sexual Explorations

In upper primary school I covertly read the iconic book on women's sexual fantasies, '*My Secret Garden*' by Nancy Friday; Mum kept it on her bedside table. My best friend Wanda and I practised kissing each other, and then on a school excursion at a local national park, hidden deep in the bush, we practised with a boy we both liked. Wanda and I started our moon-time bleeding on exactly the same day. Although she didn't believe me at the time, much later I discovered how common this is for girls and women who are close.

My parents had '*The Joy of Sex*' on our lounge bookshelf. They gave us thorough sex education instruction when we entered puberty. To explore our yoni, it was suggested that we use a carrot and lubrication, which I excitedly did with my stepsister Jaz and best friend Wanda. I'm very grateful that my parents gave me sex education; it encouraged my self-esteem and my ability to enjoy my body, go with the flow, and also to know my boundaries – when to say 'No'. In retrospect, it was highly unusual to have this unique combination of freedom and safety.

Five Early Experiences of Healing Wounds through the Magic Wand of the Heart

1. I always wished for my parents to get back together and stop fighting. Although a reconciliation never happened, in later years they did correspond, meet, and reminisce, which really warmed my heart! Wishes can take time to manifest.

2. I used to wish upon the first star I saw in the night sky for my own horse, since I can remember, and then I was finally allowed my own pony when I was fourteen years old. It took work. From the age of nine I did hours of housework at $2 an hour in exchange for pony riding lessons. This love affair continued until I was thirty. I have had several horses and also taught a friend's daughters to ride.

3. At school, I loved playing the piano, though I was bigger on expression than technique. My stepdad coached me with my piece, Mozart variations on Twinkle, Twinkle Little Star. Thanks to his encouragement and support, I surprised everyone by giving the top performance and was awarded a scholarship, a gift of a year's tuition fees!

4. Starting university, I wished to meet a handsome medical student, and I did, at an orientation week social function. We fell in love and dated for several years (until he graduated and his family made pointed comments about my being his secretary and providing children).

5. As girls, my stepsister Jaz and I played with 'unseeable' horses and boyfriends. Mine was always called Gus. The first partner I shared a home with was called Gus. We met through an amateur theatre group, and I became stepmother to his gorgeous children for five years over holidays and alternate weekends.

Turning a Wound into a Magical Wand

After growing up, I worked hard to turn my childhood wounds into a magical wand – through becoming a social justice lawyer, doing inner work, therapy, becoming a tantric healer and mentor, learning meditation, and self-development. I believe the Universe sends bigger, more magnificent challenges to those who are up for it, and when we stop growing, we stagnate.

It is within everyone's power to take self-responsibility, to think independently, and to heal and grow our self-esteem, compassion, kindness, intuition, and inner strength muscles, despite and beyond our circumstances. Although childhood wounds leave scars, they do get less painful and patterns less controlling, the more healing work we do. Focusing on the heart and magnetising desires is so much fun! What used to really trigger me can now make me smile. When I notice myself being triggered, I'm also curious – what gold may be underneath? I see triggers as the Universe encouraging me to be more alive, powerful, self-aware, and also less concerned about what others think.

Lesson 1 – Turn your wound into a magical wand through heart healing.

Chapter 2

Wake the Fuck Up!

This chapter gives examples of things I learnt from my early years in law and life, the numerous times the Universe woke me the fuck up to put me on a more healing path. Through the healing world, I discovered Tantra.

But first, the world of conscious sexuality couldn't be further from the way I related for my first decade of adulthood. Prior to waking up, intimacy required alcohol. Single in my mid to late twenties, I hung out with bright, ambitious, attractive, feisty professional women hungry for love. On the prowl like lionesses, we worked hard by day and played hard by night. I took pride in matching my drinks with big, burly guys. (In hindsight this was insane, I'm 155cm tall!)

It was just a matter of time before there were distressing incidents I'm not proud of, which I'm sharing because I see so many young people on the path I was on.

1988 – I Discover Healing, am Woken the Fuck Up and Blown Away

I'd almost finished university, and I still recall being shocked when my mother quit her job and her second marriage and moved to Sydney to study natural therapies. She started doing yoga and massage, eating brown rice, drinking herbal tea, taking breathwork journeys, and recalling her past lives. I worried she'd lost the plot and was off the planet.

Then Mum introduced me to Louise Hay's book, '*You Can Heal Your Life*', when I was about twenty years old, which I am so grateful for. Through learning to do affirmations, speaking my feelings, and journalling, as suggested in *You Can Heal Your Life*, I was able to rid myself of the chronic debilitating sore throats I'd had since childhood.

1991 – I Almost Burn Down the Supreme Court (a Heritage Building), which Wakes Me the Fuck Up!

After my Mum moved to Sydney, I completed my final year of uni and got my first full-time job as a Supreme Court Judge's Associate. I moved in with a girlfriend who was heavily into drinking, partying, and smoking green weed. I sat in Court for most of a year listening to mostly dull, dry legal appeals and struggled to stay awake. (If anyone has insomnia, I recommend a legal podcast; lawyers' voices can be very soporific!) I popped out of Court to put a pie in the oven, went back, and forgot about it… a secretary walking past found the oven on fire! She gave me such a tongue-lashing for almost burning down the building – I was so abashed.

In starting work for a legal aid firm in a poorer end of town, I knew I needed more skills for the personal and professional challenges I had on my plate. I enrolled in psychology, became a Lifeline Telephone Crisis Counsellor, and joined an amateur theatre group – though nothing could really prepare me for the culture shock I experienced.

1992 – Gus and his Kids Wake Me the Fuck Up

Through the theatre group, I met Gus, a sweet divorcee with two boys, aged four and six, whom I fell in love with at first sight. They both had long wavy hair, one blonde, one brunette, big personalities, and a great sense of humour.

We bought a Volkswagen Kombi camper van that we enjoyed many holidays in. It was always breaking down; one time I had to get a Supreme Court appeal adjourned to another date as we were stuck in a remote location waiting for a repair.

My work was stressful. Having the boys around was very good for me. Once, when I was tired and overworked, I accidentally broke a glass, and Dougie, the youngest, went out and surprised me with flowers from the garden, an adorable and loving gesture.

I Wake the Fuck Up and Make Peace with My Parents

Gus keenly observed that my mother's calls made me uncomfortable and that I avoided her. My stepsister Jaz, a child psychologist, recommended a book called *'Making Peace with Your Adult Children'* to clear childhood PTSD, and Mum organised to fly over and stay for a few days to do healing work together. I still remember the feelings of emotional vulnerability. This time was significant in bringing us closer together. I also saw a psychologist, Sue, who I referred clients to for court reports. My clients were poor, on welfare, anti-social, and extremely mistrustful of authority figures, but they liked and trusted Sue. I saw her three times, and her professional opinion was childhood neglect. Therapy and the 'Making Peace' workbook helped me to move past the block and open my heart to my mother. They made me more mindful of the ways we self-medicate, and I was able to take baby steps towards healing.

Clients Wake Me the Fuck Up – There but by the Grace of God Go I

In working with clients on legal aid and from different cultural backgrounds, my motto became 'There but by the Grace of

God go I' – after hearing story after story of multi-generational abuse. If I'd grown up in their shoes, I'd no doubt be popping out as many kids as possible, collecting welfare, feeding my kids junk food, who'd be running amok. I'd be open to shadier ways of making money, and self-medicating, using what I could to numb the pain and chaos of life. The average educational level of people in prison is grade 6, with a reading level of a 10–12-year-old. Most prison inmates are from highly disadvantaged backgrounds, and most abusers have themselves been abused by an older parent figure, relative, or so-called friend. Yet the legal system fails to recognise inter-generational abuse; it just tries to manage and put a Band-Aid or superficial plaster on the symptoms.

I Wake the Fuck Up and Learn How Law Works

My first cases were ones where clients went to prison, and the Court decided whether they would get to keep or see their kids. If there was a chance the client could go to prison, I'd tell them to bring their toothbrush to Court. I learnt to find out which Magistrate was sitting on the bench before deciding how to handle and pitch the case. Luckily my senior colleagues and court staff were mostly very kind and helpful. People imagine that lawyers are wise and successful because they read a lot; however, the best lawyers, in my experience, are also very intuitive.

The Worst Thing that's Ever Happened, which Woke Me the Fuck Up

With work and life stresses, I partied too hard one night, had way too much alcohol and marijuana, and foolishly drove in the wee hours of the morning. I came in the driveway too fast. It was very dark, and I didn't see my beloved cat Ziggy run down the driveway. She was a beautiful, sweet, grey fluffy only a year old. In shock at the emergency vet, I felt so sick to my stomach and fought not to bring up its contents. They had to put her down.

After this I realised that although it was awful, it could have been much worse; I could have killed a person and gone to prison for life.

1995 – Sexual Incapacity Claims Wake Me the Fuck Up to Law as a Cultural Narrative

In law we call it 'creative instruction taking', and there was no better example of this than claims of sexual incapacity. I worked for a litigious plaintiff personal injury firm that reminded me of Robin Hood, taking from the rich so that their clients, who were usually poor non-native, English-speaking migrants, would benefit. In the early to mid-nineties, they had more appeals to the State Supreme and High Courts than any other firm.

Litigation is a common tactic used by defendants with deep pockets, such as personal injury insurance companies; the law of averages means that on balance they achieve more favourable settlements because the opposition considers how much it will cost them in legal fees to dispute the case.

The firm invented a new head of damage, 'loss of sexual capacity,' that made a huge amount of money. When a client had a permanent injury, it was my job to know the sexual positions they likely could and couldn't engage in, so we could suggest that due to their injury, their sexual positions and frequency must be limited. All the clients had to do was nod their heads in response to our 'creative instruction-taking'. The only 'proof' required was a psychiatric report from a friendly pro-plaintiff doctor. I still remember the day the government closed this loophole and how upsetting it was for that firm to lose all that business!

I Wake the Fuck Up and Explore Spirituality

Outwardly I had achieved everything I needed: a promotion and good, stable job, a loving partner, step-children, friends, and an active social life. But inside I felt something was lacking. By that time, Gus had retrained as a school teacher, was loving it, and was posted to a remote country school, meaning we only saw each other one weekend every few months.

With Gus away, I got into exploring the Theosophical Society, learnt astral travelling, tried rebirthing breathwork, and experienced my first incredible spiritual awakenings. During my first breathwork session, I received strong guidance from my Higher Self. I saw blue skies and green hills on my 'mind screen' and knew I needed to move to the country for a better life.

I got a job easily as a country lawyer by the sea in a fishing farming town. The partners were lovely, and I was in charge of my own client workload. I was most excited by having the time to learn more healing techniques: reiki, massage, and rebirthing breathwork, which is where I first heard of Tantra.

1998-99 – Rebirther Training Wakes Me the Fuck Up

At the age of twenty-nine, I decided to commit to rebirther teacher training. Rebirthing, or breathwork therapy, is an ecstatic gateway to the subconscious. It creates energy in the body and is detoxing. I use this incredible transformational tool regularly in life, moving the body to music or in the bath, and in tantric journeying.

This training meant flying to the city on alternate weekends for four months, and staying with friends. It was a big commitment and one I enjoyed very much. The kundalini (life-force) energy raised by conscious connected breathing for an hour led to some fascinating results. In one rebirthing session, my friend Linda spoke with a French accent, recounting a past life during WW2, and her accent disappeared right after the session!

Clearing Wakes Me the Fuck Up: Touch Assist and Learning from a Navy Seal

Breathwork led me to another modality called Clearing. At a Clearing communication workshop, I met the gorgeous man who was to become my first husband, Adam. Clearing is a modality that uses a device like a lie detector test to measure the sweat glands on the palms in order to delve just under the conscious mind but not too deep. This device is also used in Scientology, but Clearing practitioners say they use the technology in a more ethical way. One of the techniques we learnt was called 'touch assist.' With touch assist, when you have a minor accident, say you stub your toe, what you do is hold your sore toe onto the thing you tripped on, and feel the vibrations move through the injured body part, and breathe. If you burn yourself, turn off the iron or stove and wait until it cools down of course, and then do it. This is a good way of accelerating the healing process. I and many others have benefitted greatly from this technique.

Adam and I embarked on a huge adventure together, travelling to the UK and many other countries. In the UK I discovered Tantra. Little was I to know then, that I would become a tantric healer and the UK would become my home for the next twelve years.

During my first year in London, I did a second round of rebirther training, now in the Lakes District, with Colin Sisson, whose story is interesting. Colin is from New Zealand, was drafted to fight in the Vietnam War, and became an army SEAL, a special operative. He claims that rebirthing saved his life, as after the war many of his former colleagues died of PTSD and the chemical weapon Agent Orange.

1999-2000 – World Travel Wakes Me the Fuck Up

Adam and I spent five months in North, Central, and South America, back-packing. We loved California, Las Vegas, the Grand Canyon – the usual tourist spots. But I became really obsessed with the ancient ruins we saw in Southern Mexico, Guatemala, and Peru. We bussed from Mexico City to Guatemala, went to Spanish school in the mountains, then flew to Honduras to go scuba diving, before flying to Lima, Peru. I can still recall how amazing it felt to be surrounded by local children in so-called third-world countries and hand out fruit, which to us cost very little. How word spread and then more children came for food – travelling out of one's comfort zone really puts things in perspective, and makes me so grateful for life's opportunities!

In Peru we had our coco leaves read by a traditional healer. She told me that I had healing gifts which I should develop to work as a healer. Adam asked about his dream to commercialise hemp, which is a wonder product, a natural fibre of great strength that has been used since ancient civilisation for fabrics and ropes. Hemp powder is a superfood, the oil and seeds have high nutritional content. The healer told Adam that his dream to work in hemp would take a long time to be a commercial success, and this dampened his enthusiasm.

In South America I read Graham Hancock's book '*Fingerprints of the Gods*', about mysterious advanced civilisations that had risen and fallen. The incredible Nazca lines were such an example – huge shapes of plants, birds, and a monkey, that could only be seen properly or in entirety from flying over them in a small plane. Although Graham Hancock has continued to write books on his theories and discoveries, supported by archaeologists and geologists like Gregg Braden, they have not found favour with the mainstream. I can still recall the eerie sensation as we took in these incredible monuments in the middle of a tropical forest, the sound of howler monkeys like lions roaring, and butterflies twirling. The amazing pyramids were often off the beaten track, difficult to get to. I became hooked on exploring ancient ruins, and in later years I took several trips to the Middle East and Asia to take in the magic of the wonders of the world: Egypt, Cambodia, Jordan, Israel, Hue, Tao City, Vietnam, Red Sea Coast.

My love of exploring travel, healing, and ancient ruins led me to strike up conversations and friendships with people from different backgrounds all over the world, and made me realise that despite our different backgrounds, **we are one big human family**. I was shocked to learn through one of my Spanish teachers that Guatemala had been invaded by America, who sought political control several times for conditions favourable for the American United Fruit Company. Facts I hadn't learnt at uni or heard on the news in Australia. The waking up I did in those years taught me to be incredibly humble – so grateful to experience the beauty, remarkable landscapes, and people outside the confines of Western culture.

Lesson 2 – Wake the fuck up – the Universe is speaking. Are you listening?

Chapter 3

Gratitude for the Silver Lining

I've had four major accidents in my life, all were traumatic. These were both the worst and best times of my life.

Two accidents were on my bike. I broke my arm on day 1 of a Tantric Journey training in Thailand, and another time, had a car accident where my car was written off. After all four accidents, I went to hospital with significant injuries. These experiences taught me that there's always a higher power looking out for us – even if it doesn't seem that way. It showed me how important it is to always be grateful for the silver lining in the cloud.

The First Accident – Summer 1988

The first accident happened when I was twenty. I'd achieved my life goals of getting to law school, being elected to student politics, and dating a gorgeous medical student. However, nothing turned out like I expected! My relationship was on the rocks, I hated the shifting alliance manipulations and intrigues of student politics, law school was a bore and a drag. The biggest excitement was planning social events like the annual university ball. And occasional unexpected thrills, like one day in class when the lecturer paused and my friend 'whispered' loudly, "What colour briefcase will you have when you graduate?" There was a pause and the whole class burst out laughing. Life mostly felt like a tedious treadmill, having all the excitement of watching paint dry.

My first accident caused the most serious injuries – a car door swiped me off my bike on a hot summer's day. I was knocked onto the kerb, breathless, my leg was bleeding and swollen. The young couple took me home. I nearly fainted with the pain and shock but didn't want to make a fuss.

I stayed in hospital for two days with a haematoma or large multi-coloured bruise from mid-thigh to my foot, stitches on my knee, and I still have a dent on my calf to this day, from hitting the kerb.

I was released from hospital with a large bandage on my knee and a limp. The physio told me I walked like a duck!

After the accident I quit student politics, broke up with my medical student boyfriend, and made a decision that anything over 50% was wasted effort for subjects I didn't care for. It was like the accident gave me new strength of purpose to make better decisions for greater satisfaction.

After graduating as a lawyer, I filled my life with other activities which were fulfilling.

I took a course in women's self-defence, taught by a black-belt in Taekwondo, and was amazed to learn the simple techniques that don't require a lot of strength and that have been successfully deployed by children. Things like use of voice and a knee or nose strike, that made me feel a lot more confident and independent.

The extra-curricular activities I did gave me a lot of joy. One such activity was amateur theatre, performing in English-style comedy dramas, murder mysteries, and Christmas pantomimes... where you got dressed up in costume, there was a villain and heroine, and the audience participated, shouting things like, "Watch out, he's behind you!" "Oh yes he is… oh no he's not!"

The Second Accident – A Rural Coastal Town, 1998

The second bike accident happened when I was twenty-nine, in a small country Australian fishing and farming town. I'd declined a partnership in the law firm I worked in, as my heart and Soul weren't in it, though the people and lifestyle were wonderful. I loved doing relaxation massage, reiki, and rebirther training, had three horses, regularly took a friend's two daughters horse riding, and surfed with friends. I had changed a lot on the inside, but outwardly, my life hadn't changed. It was stagnating.

This accident was also caused by a car door opening, and this time I knew EXACTLY what to do to heal. Instead of hiding my feelings, I expressed them openly, cried, called, and prayed for support. Miraculously, a kind angel was nearby, who held my hand until the ambulance arrived and called healer friends, who immediately sent me reiki healing, and the local health food shop, who sent arnica, a homeopathic remedy for bruising, in a taxi to the hospital (they later refused to accept any payment for it!) I knew the ambulance officers who took me to hospital. Another healer friend came to the hospital, held my hand, fed me ice chips, and went through x-rays with me. Instead of having to remain in hospital for a day or two, I was taken care of by a reiki master friend who gave me healing and fed me delicious soups, and I knew that thanks to all the healing support, I would recover without lasting injuries.

After the accident I realised I had all this joy and skills from the healing modalities I'd learned, but I wasn't doing much to pursue this passion, except my voluntary breathwork case studies. (These included a secretary in the law business, who ended up retraining as a naturopath, marrying my cousin, raising children, and growing veggies!)

While I was recuperating from the accident, I gave my notice at work and made a decision to travel to the UK.

Shortly after the accident was when I met Adam, who was also planning to travel to London for a working holiday at the end of the year. After we started dating, Adam told me he'd wished on an American Indian Intention Feather, for me to call him. Even more weirdly, he told me on our second date that I'd be married and pregnant by the time I was thirty-two – and he ended up being right.

Moving to London and Exploring New Worlds, February 1999

Moving to London, where all the healing modalities in the world were at my fingertips, I felt like a kid in a lolly shop! After a year of travelling adventures, I joined and then taught at an international energy healing school. It was a real-life Harry Potter existence, we went to the school by train, which left from Paddington Station in London.

London was a real eye-opener. In the small Australian country town I'd moved from, there was only one traffic light for a pedestrian crossing.

The first time I caught a London bus, the driver was a woman dressed as a goth with heavy black make-up, heeled boots, and multiple piercings, and she drove that bus like a bat out of hell!

I later became an energy and tantric healer, offering sessions in London and Bristol.

The Third Accident – at Tantra School, Tao Garden, Thailand, July 2016

The third accident happened in Thailand, where I travelled with a friend to retrain with my tantric journey teacher from London. Twelve years after he trained me one-on-one, he'd set up a school and worked with groups. Unfortunately, my accident happened on the day I arrived at the resort. It was wet season in the tropics. I was barefoot, chatting with others on my course, when I slipped and broke my wrist.

Luckily, the King of Thailand had spared no expense setting up a first-world health system, and I hardly had to wait to be treated. I re-joined the class and gave massages with my one good arm and my other elbow, using my body weight. The massage was performed on a futon on the floor, and included walking up and down the body, which my teacher, a short Sri Lankan man with a huge smile, did effortlessly. Most of us required a walking frame to keep our balance. I continued to do qigong exercises each morning and evening, modifying them to suit me. I also had saunas and massages, and sat in the pool, leaving my plastered arm out of the water.

Although I was devastated to not fully participate, I benefitted greatly from living near the resort for a couple of months. The locals got to know me and were very kind. They sold me street food at local prices, and I hired a push bike to get around.

Once I discovered that Thai people don't traditionally plaster their breaks due to risks of tendon adhesion, which can cause long-term side effects, I had my plaster removed early and had regular healing treatments, including from a kick-boxing practitioner who was used to treating broken bones. All of this ensured I recovered without any permanent damage.

After my arm healed, I flew to London for an intense week of practising Tao Tantric massages with a few of my classmates from all over the world. The massages were practised on volunteers who paid reduced rates. It was a beautiful, crazy week of Tantra boot camp. We stayed in the London apartments together and gave two massages per day, each session up to three or four hours long. We met each day for meals and discussed our sessions. Participating was a rare privilege and gift, it helped strengthen my arm and develop myself as a practitioner. After this week, I stayed with another practitioner for a few days and gave sessions, including sessions to a trans-gender man with a prosthetic.

After London, I visited friends at a small permaculture[3] community (permaculture means permanent agriculture) near the border of Scotland, where I continued to give healing massages and gardened, strengthening my arm. Highlights of this trip were visiting picture-book pretty towns dotted with op shops (thrift shops) filled with books and armchairs, and chilly autumn swimming in the River Wye.

My London teacher published a book[4] with numerous client case studies, including of a woman who flew to London from Saudi Arabia with her driver on shopping trips and visited him. The first time she wore a full burka, the second time she removed part of her veil, etc. – the clothing doesn't matter because the massage is profoundly deep, and the client chooses the level of intimacy they are comfortable with.

---

[3] What is permaculture? – Permaculture College Australia

[4] Emotional Detox Through Bodywork: A Woman's Guide to Healing and Awakening, Mal Weeraratne, https://www.amazon.com.au/Emotional-Detox-Through-Bodywork-Awakening/dp/1504994159

Tantric Healing Massage Goes Off in Iceland, October 2016

My friend invited me to Iceland for a week and I gave massage treatments, which were very popular, in her attic. While in Reykjavík, I saw the Northern Lights, bathed in the Hot Pot (volcanically heated outdoor pools with an incredible variety of temperatures), was gifted a bus trip to some glorious waterfalls, a spectacular volcanic black-sand beach, and a glacier. Healing work is extremely popular in Iceland, they're open-minded people.

But for the accident where I broke my arm, I would not have stayed in Thailand for two months and experienced all the wonderful healing treatments. And probably would not have continued onto the UK and Iceland.

After I returned to Australia, I set up my second tantric healing business and had the privilege to again witness incredible positive changes in clients.

To strengthen my arm and challenge myself, I started physical training with army women. I found them so encouraging, positive. A tantric friend I used to swap massages with taught me to run like a ninja, an efficient way to run.

The Fourth Accident – A Hot Summer's Day after Ninja Training, February 2018

The fourth accident was in my car when I was forty-eight years old. I'd just done ninja training with army women. It was over 40 degrees, I felt nauseous as I'd had nothing but a coffee and was late to meet a friend for a workout. A car came out of a side street, and my car was written off. The worst was calling my elderly Mum to bring my ID to the accident scene and her shock at my mangled car. In hospital I kept up my deep breathing and affirming healing to my body, knowing that there was a reason for the accident, even if I didn't know it yet.

After this accident, I was lucky to have friends invite me to stay, cheering me up no end, cooking delicious meals, and doing gentle healing yoga together. I had difficulty getting back into a car and driving, but I did on my doctor's advice to prevent post-traumatic stress disorder. Of course, the reason for the accident was to get me away from the extreme army fitness scene, not a supportive place long-term for a tantric lawyer! And I was propelled to act more in line with my core values.

After the accident I quit army training and was inspired to take up the challenge of being a car-free, peaceful, eco-warrior for two-and-a-half years. I used public transport, bought a push-bike as my main form of transport, and sometimes took taxis or Ubers. I was disappointed by the settlement delays as the insurance companies fought over liability, ironic after working in this industry.

After the accident, I connected more with like-minded people and went on an amazing trip to Vietnam for an eco-tourism project with a majestic Taoist ruined city. The city felt strangely familiar. It contained many ancient sacred sexuality symbols, and I had 'past life memories'.

I also booked myself into an International School of Temple Arts (ISTA) course in Sydney and organised an epic roadtrip with a friend for my 50th birthday. It was incredible.

I'm so grateful to the silver lining in all these accidents. Their purpose was to wake me up, to realign my life direction with my highest soul path.

Lesson 3 – You are always on your highest soul path. If you stray, the Universe will send you a realignment opportunity in the form of a challenge.

When the Universe whispers, we need to listen – it can feel at first like a tickle from a feather, then if we don't listen, it can feel like an apple thrown at the head, escalating to a Mack truck or a Concord!

Chapter 4

Where there's a Will, there's a Way

How this mantra enabled me to follow my dream of becoming a healer at 'a modern Hogwarts' International School of Magic

After Adam and I had been overseas for a year, we enrolled in the School of Energy Healing together, the most thorough training that was available. Multiple modalities and levels of the energy field were explored, with appropriate healing methods and techniques for each aspect of consciousness. Equal emphasis was placed on practitioner development, a process of rigorous self-inquiry and personal healing. It was a deep, life changing experience and I felt that I had found my purpose.[5]

Sadly, Adam dropped out after a class, deciding it wasn't for him. I stayed and wanted to complete the three-year training. There were obstacles, it was expensive, but I managed to get a study visa and numerous part-time jobs: a receptionist in a South Kensington hotel, tutor to the hotel owner's children, a masseuse, and delivering sandwiches on a bike to office workers. Yet no matter how hard I worked, financially it was very tough. A stroke of luck happened, Adam was sponsored by his company, we married, and I got work as a lawyer, initially in a local council, defending claims of personal injury and property damage, then for the Treasury Solicitor.

---

[5] Co-founded by Marc Blausten (plymouthfunctionalmedicineclinic.co.uk)

Will comes into our life and shows us that where there's a will, there's a way

The unexpected occurred – we got pregnant – by accident. I used a natural method from Boots to take my temperature, which I had doubts about. I'd stopped using the contraceptive pill for health reasons and hadn't yet discovered the honeycap. Adam and I loved each other very much but knew after two years living together that we wanted very different things in life. I made a tough decision, knowing then that I wanted to be a healer more than anything, including being a mother.

I started speaking with the Soul who came into my body to find out why he'd come and to send unconditional love and healing. He told me his name was Will, and his message to me was, 'Where there's a Will, there's a Way'. He said it was not my highest soul path to settle down, have a child, and buy a home with Adam, but to have faith and trust in myself and my love of healing. And to not allow anything to get in the way. He came knowing that his stay would be brief on the Earth plane, and once his Soul had delivered this message about my life purpose, it was complete.

It wasn't easy – being pregnant made me emotional and sensitive. Sound healing week at healing school was torture! Later I saw a Harley Street gynaecologist who helped women use a natural form of contraceptive, a honey cap – a smaller type of diaphragm kept in a jar of honey, a natural contraceptive. She told me that she operated under secrecy, her medical colleagues did not approve of her prescribing these for women, honey being a natural product, and the medical industry preferring to promote chemical products with a higher profit margin.

A Lesson of Faith and Trust

This motto kept me going in London when I wasn't sure how I would be able to stay, when money ran low. There were times when I was very grateful to sleep on a friend's couch or a camping mattress on the floor, applying for various visas – it's truly a miracle that I managed to stay in the UK for twelve years, on and off. I'm very grateful to Adam and all who helped me to follow my dreams to stay in the UK.

The six years I spent at the healing school were the culmination of lifelong dreams that involved making significant sacrifices and showed me that where there is a will, there is a way for dreams to come true. I also have to thank so many friends and family who supported me with kindness.

There were plenty of times over the years when I didn't listen to the soft voice of intuition due to fear, mostly fear of being poor, fear of what might happen if I didn't conform to expectations of society, work, my partner, friends, and family. The many times I didn't listen led to accidents. The more I learnt to tune in and fully trust my intuition, the more I discovered how truly abundant the world is, what an infinite number of choices we have in life, and how important it is to match my vibration with the most desirable outcome.

Where there's a Will, there's a Way to Follow Dreams and Intuition

The teachers of the School of Energy Healing (SEH) were a couple, both homeopaths who had completed the 4-year Barbara Brennan School programme in the United States. They added pieces to the curriculum like naturopathy, medical qigong (slow martial arts, like Tai Chi), 5Rhythms dance, core energetics (body-oriented psychotherapy), and of course,

Tantra. They'd facilitated several Tantra training courses and introduced techniques for circulation of sexual energy and chakra-breathing. These practices assisted us as practitioners to heal others without feeling drained.

The school met for five weeks per year near the Lakes District at a delightful guest house in a picturesque town called Mickleton. The first year of the training was an introduction to energy, the first three levels of the energy field: physical, emotional, and mental.

Each week had a particular theme or technique we worked with. In the first year, one week was devoted to sound healing – using our voices as healing tools, which influence the body. There is a true story of monks at a monastery who spent a lot of time in devotional singing and chanting. The monastery got a new abbot who decided to cut down the singing and chanting and increased the workload of the monks. They started to get ill. Meat was introduced to their vegetarian diet, but it didn't help. Eventually the abbot brought back the singing and chanting as he realised it made the monks strong, healthy, and happy.

The second year of the School of Energy Healing (the one I later taught on) was transformation, the astral level: inner child, clearing astral clouds, objects, past lives, and entities – it was a lot of drama and fun. The third year was the fifth level (the energy field template, divine level within, or blueprint, which looks like the negative of a photo[6]). Psychic surgery, the sixth (angelic). And the seventh was the monad or God level (connection to all that is).

It made me so happy to have the opportunity to live in London and immerse myself in the healing world for several years – that

____

[6] Etheric Template Body: Fifth Layer of the Human Energy Field

world is all about developing intuition. Staying in the UK after Adam left and went back to Australia in early 2002 required a lot of trust. Over and over again, I had to lean into the fear of taking on this huge commitment. Adam used to say, "Use the force". I would breathe deeply on the plane and surrender the outcome, being okay with the worst possible scenario of being refused entry at the airport and having to return to Australia. I was surprised how things worked out for me, obtaining various visas, jobs, and homes.

I See My Stepdad Before He Passes – March 2002

For several months I had a feeling that all wasn't well with my stepdad. Then I received a message, he had pancreatic cancer, which was terminal. He didn't have long. The next day I booked a flight back to Australia. While I was in the air, he was in surgery, the cancer couldn't be removed.

I did energy healing on him and sent love to his pancreas, not to heal the cancer but to prepare his Soul to leave the Earth plane. He was amazed, felt the healing was fantastic and that I'd gone beyond the world he knew about, which is what children are supposed to do. It was so incredibly affirming and beautiful yet bitter-sweet, sad, knowing I would miss his wisdom, which he said was now within me, feeling closer than we ever had before.

Just after I returned to London, I received a call from his partner that he had passed. That precious time together in his final days is something I am forever grateful for.

Lesson 4 – Where there's a will, there's a way – Life's not all unicorns shitting glitter and rainbows – when you follow your heart and truth, and trust in the path, let go, the Universe often supports you!

Chapter 5

More Multiple Orgasms Please!

How Orgasms Stopped a War

My Tantra teacher tells a story of a war between clans, a war that lasted for decades. Women became tired of losing their husbands, sons, brothers, and fathers to endless cycles of war. The argument had been going on for so long that no one even remembered what it was about. The women from opposite sides got together and decided to put an end to it. They made a collective decision that until and unless all the men stopped fighting, there would be no more sex for them. When faced with this ultimatum, the men on both sides decided to make peace!

Exploring Open-relating

My introduction to conscious open-relating began in London after Adam left the UK and I moved in with a female housemate, Evie, who was a year ahead of me at the School of Energy Healing. Evie and I meditated together to get a picture of our ideal flat before we found it.

One night we went to a 5Rhythms conscious dance class, connected with two gorgeous guys, and brought them home. I'll call them Fred and Sam. I ended up with Fred, he was a nice dancer, and we had an erotic dance… However that experience taught me that when a man peaks too quickly and it's 'All Over Red Rover' while his lady is just getting warmed up, it can be a very frustrating experience. It becomes a true tragedy if the lady is trapped in an unhappy situation she simply can't get away from. Which is far more common than you might think.

Fred's lingam was small – but size is no predictor either for a wonderful or dull night in the bedroom – in fact one of my most incredible lovers was not particularly well-endowed but has so many other wonderful qualities, and we are still friends to this day.

Fred was very sweet, made good eye contact, but after a tiny climax that reminded me of a squeaking rodent, I was not keen to repeat the experience with him. Having said this, there is of course a happy medium here. I had a lover later whom I'd met at an Osho community gathering. He insisted on screaming the house down, roaring like a bear for an extended length of time…

The MOST Comforting and Healing Tantric Massage of My Life – 2002

I found myself connecting with Sam a few weeks later. The thing about open-relating is that there are a myriad of possibilities, and that's what makes life so interesting. We decided to do a massage swap. It happened to be my moon time, and I suggested we postpone but Sam wasn't put off. He had been brought up in a conscious community where this was welcomed and celebrated.

Lovely Sam understood that when a woman is bleeding she can still enjoy comfort, consideration, stroking, complete acceptance, and… receiving pleasure! It's challenging for me to share this vulnerable experience as it remains, to this day, one of the most intimate moments of my life. Sam was unconcerned about soiling his white t-shirt, wiping his hands on it, AND… after a couple of hours of ecstasy in which every muscle in my body was loose and I had so many endorphins flowing through my system… relaxed as a pussycat in the sun… HE CAUGHT A BUS HOME AFTERWARDS – AND HE REFUSED MY OFFER TO BORROW A CLEAN T-SHIRT!

What an amazing guy. There was my healing.

Alice Down the Tantric Rabbit-hole – Summer 2003

After I finished my energy healing training, I decided to take a series of sessions with a London-based tantric journey practitioner, who helps women to experience ejaculation by releasing layers of trauma and numbness stored in the body. It was the most incredible experience. Although I'd always been orgasmic since I was a child, I'd never experienced the let-go of female ejaculation. It feels like peeing but when you taste it, it's a different substance – yet to be analysed by medical science, known for centuries in India as 'amrita', nectar of life in Sanskrit, one of the world's oldest languages.

The detailed pre-session questionnaire was intimate and confronting. At the beginning of my first session, we chatted over a cup of herbal tea. Then I went for a sauna, followed by a kundalini shaking meditation and full-body massage – two hours on my back, an hour on my front – by which time I was soooo relaxed. Permission was requested to go into my yoni, which felt a bit numb. I was reassured that this was quite normal. After a couple more sessions I discovered new sensations in my yoni, and strong emotions were released – fear, anger, and sadness. After a couple more sessions inside my yoni felt more pleasurable and orgasmic, also incredibly WILDER, much more alive.

In subsequent sessions, my teacher encouraged and trained me one-on-one to become a tantric practitioner. He showed me how in tantric lovemaking, the man waits for the woman's yoni to become ready and invites his lingam in when it is half erect, which feels more like a friend knocking at the back door than a stranger forcefully entering the front. He taught me how to help men control ejaculation and become multiply orgasmic, for them to in-jaculate. By helping them open their hearts, emote, and move energy through their bodies, this practice assists men to be more energetic and match women's sexual desires, so couples can enjoy both ecstasy and deeper intimacy for longer periods of time.

I was completely fascinated. I practised the techniques on myself and on open friends from my healing and 5Rhythms conscious dance communities. I am so grateful to this day to every being, friend and client, who trusted me enough to say yes to the experience. It was a journey down the rabbit-hole, and I was Alice, discovering magical worlds. The feeling was comparable to learning to pilot a sports car or a rocket. The particular challenge from a tantric therapist's perspective is holding a professional, detached yet heart-centred space.

Tantric practices create expansion and liberation beyond the body-mind personality, the tantric worldview sees all material reality as animated by unlimited divine power. I'd long been fascinated with but had not understood traditional Tantra. Ancient scriptures and statues depict Hindu goddesses and gods entwining violent and erotic power. There's tension and exploration of opposing destructive and creative material forces in life. In Asia, tantric Buddhas smile enigmatically as they watch the unending wheel of samsara, or karma, without reacting to high and low points in life. Modern or Neo-Tantra features energy orgasms, teaches how to follow one's ecstatic current, is exploratory and disconnected from religion or dogma.

For some people, Taoism means becoming a sexual ninja, men can benefit from separating orgasm from ejaculation, and can even learn to lift coke cans with their genitals! Women are encouraged to use yoni eggs internally to activate and tighten their pelvic floor muscles, female Tao adepts can even spin the eggs internally.

Home of the Druids and Priestesses – Magical Glastonbury, Summer 2004

After I graduated from the three-year School of Energy Healing training, I was asked to return as a teacher. A fellow student, Jim, invited me to visit his hometown of Glastonbury, a very spiritual area in the south-west of England set on ley lines, called dragon lines, similar to song lines of Australia. The area features mysterious crop and stone circles, forests, and caves reputed to have been the legendary magician Merlin's home. This has inspired many stories, such as 'The Mists of Avalon' by Marion Zimmer Bradley, which portrayed Glastonbury as the home of Druids and Priestesses of Avalon since the beginning of time, with links to the ancient civilisations of Atlantis and Lemuria.[7]

Law was very different in pre-industrial Celtic Britannia, administered by Priestesses and Druids. Druid means one who knows, a strong seer, one who is wise, true, firm, and steadfast, magician or sorcerer.[8] Druids were the learned class of teachers, judges, and priests. They resolved disputes, judged outcomes, and fixed penalties. 'They studied ancient verse, natural philosophy, astronomy, and the lore of the gods, some spending as much as twenty years in training.'[9] In Celtic culture, women were also druids, priests, battle leaders, diviners and judges, their status was equal, sometimes even exalted compared to men, much higher than in Greek and Roman society. Law was based on an understanding of reincarnation; the Soul is journeying in a body to learn lessons in the Earth school or playground. I think this perspective is far preferable as it deeply

---

[7] https://www.amazon.com/Mists-Avalon-Marion-Zimmer-Bradley/dp/0345350499
[8] Online Etymology Dictionary
[9] Encyclopaedia Britannica Online

resonates and it requires humans to be more responsible and consider their behaviour over longer timespans.

Anglo-Saxon law included an awareness of the spiritual dimension, that life was not a completely random experience, but a complex, interlocking tapestry in which we are all connected by threads, confirmed by a growing number of quantum scientists.[10] The Magna Carta, the earliest foundational English legal document for democratic societies, in Runnymeade, a place well-known in Anglo-Saxon history as a royal divination site. Now an island off the coast of England, it was a part of the mainland and literally means a place for casting of the runes, and still features a sacred yew tree which is reputed to be approximately 2,500 years old.

Law in Celtic Britannia was based on an understanding of energy – 'the Anglo-Saxon word 'haulu'…was like a generalised life-force…the source of all vitality. In a person it was believed to be generated in the head and flowed like a stream of light into the marrow of the spine and from there into the limbs and crevices of the body. [11] Parallels are seen in the concept of 'chi' in China, 'prana' in India.

Goddess Conference – Glastonbury, July 2004

I booked to stay in Glastonbury for a week of a summer Goddess Conference, hundreds of women from all over the world gathered and took over the town. I did a body-painting workshop, my chest and breasts were painted in blue Celtic spirals that were so beautiful, I decided to leave the paint on and my top off for the rest of the day. I was amazed that I didn't receive any ogling or a single sexually harassing comment. The local men

---

[10] eg Ervin Laszlo, The Self-Actualizing Cosmos: The Akasha Revolution in Science and Human Consciousness, David Bohm, Fritjof Capra, Nassim Haramein.
[11] Bates, The Real Middle-Earth pp.113-114

in Glastonbury were respectful and honoured the celebration. With the other women, we sang Goddess chants honouring the seasons, songs which had probably been sung for thousands of years on that land. Climbing the steps to the Glastonbury Tor, the distinctive hill with a Church at the top, felt weirdly familiar.

Jim showed me special sacred places in Glastonbury, introduced me to the oldest oak trees, Gog and Magog, possibly two thousand years old,[12] most of the oak trees having been deliberately cut down by the Romans when they invaded, in order to break the power of the Druids, the indigenous folk.

During that summer in Glastonbury, I started doing weather magic. I would ask for it to be fine weather while I went outside to do rituals on the Tor, go to the Chalice Well Gardens, or pick blackberries. More often than not, the weather did cooperate. I would surrender totally to whether or not it did, telling the weather that I would be able to adore nature more and send her healing and love, up close and personal. Maybe it's my imagination, but it did seem to get less rainy when I did this prayer.

First Tantric Lovemaking Experience – Glastonbury, 2004

Jim and I became lovers, it was my first experience of tantric lovemaking. We raised sexual kundalini energy through the friction and breath, then stopped for a bit while it dissipated, rather than going over the edge into ejaculation. In that way we had many orgasms. Orgasm and ejaculation are two different things, but most people think they are the same and experience them together. Women take on average about 45 minutes to

---

[12] Gog & Magog - Pilgrimage in Glastonbury (unitythroughdiversity.org); Glastonbury, the British town where druids commune with trees (lemonde.fr)

warm up to intercourse, and men a mere few seconds. Many women don't learn to enjoy sex because they aren't fully aroused when they are penetrated.

When we returned to the healing school I was promoted into a teaching role, but that meant Jim and I could not continue our relationship. Some other teachers had crossed this boundary and the fall-out was messy.

I Set Up My First Tantric Healing Business – Winter 2004

That winter I took advantage of cheap flights to holiday to the Red Sea Coast in Egypt and sat next to an English champion free-diver on the plane home. He'd heard of me and wanted to learn Tantra. In exchange, he helped me set up my first Tantric Healing website.

I soon had Tantric Healing practices in Bristol, Bath, London (Notting Hill and Kings Cross), and later, after I returned to Australia, I travelled to different cities where I saw clients (and caught up with family and friends).

I helped many clients, it was so rewarding to support someone go from depression, suicidal thoughts, serious health and relationship issues, feeling so stuck – to freedom, health, new love relationships, falling more deeply in love with their partner. Some clients suffered from premature ejaculation or were unable to orgasm.

The extent to which change occurs tends to be directly related to how committed one is to change, how much one is prepared to take on board suggestions for change, face and breathe through trauma memories and strong sensations in the body, willingness to do meditation and spiritual practices. People can actually be more resistant to pleasure than pain and numbness.

Tantra gives you a different approach to relationships. On a tantric path, you see yourself as a Soul in a body having a human journey, the purpose of life being to learn, grow, and explore being human. And what better way to do this than through relationships?

Osho Retreat Centre – Dorset, UK, 2005

At the Osho retreat centre that I visited several times, we did expressive energetic meditations and different sorts of dates were encouraged: coffee dates, dance dates, meal dates, shower dates, walk dates, cuddle dates, sleep dates… where humans attracted to each other who wished to share and explore energy could do so with mutually agreeable boundaries. For example, if a person asked you on a date (unqualified), it could involve sex, and if you like the person but not in that way, you could say no but how about a coffee date? Engaging like this requires honesty, transparency, and vulnerability, there are so many more possibilities and choices for intimacy.

Discussing the 'difficult' topics upfront, like specific desires, boundaries, other love connections, sexual health, contraception, expectations and needs afterwards, is confronting, but avoids much unhappiness down the track. It would be interesting to know how many children in the world are actually conceived consciously, deliberately, with love, desire, commitment, by people with emotional maturity and ability to parent for the next twenty years. Perhaps this one change of learning to have open, honest, upfront conversations could make a positive difference.

At the Osho Centre I connected with Roger, who introduced me to some incredible, amazing shamanic journeys in the UK. We did a lengthy fasting 'dance' in Scotland, a plant medicine circle dance, and went to Druid Camp together.[13]

I Witness a Miracle with an Ayurveda Master – Mumbai, India, 2005

A serious, earnest, dedicated trainee practitioner of Chinese medicine, Roger invited me to accompany him to a month-long Ayurvedic detox retreat in Mumbai, India, where he had permission to observe the treatment clinic. I was happy to agree.

The Ayurvedic doctor who ran the centre was Dr Pankaj Naram. Originally a Western doctor, when Dr Naram discovered Ayurveda, he had a big tummy, not much hair, and wore glasses. After learning Ayurvedic herbal medicine, he lost his gut, grew his hair back, and lost his glasses! He was well-known, footballers from Europe would fly over for adjustments, and photographs showed he treated the Dalai Lama and Mother Teresa.

There is so much information regarding the body's functioning that can be gained from pulse-taking. Ayurvedic herbs help maximise health, improve chronic conditions, and prevent illness. After taking my pulses, I was sent for tests due to a blockage in my cervix. I had been wearing a Mooncup when my pulse was taken and had forgotten to tell the doctor!

We felt privileged to watch Dr Naram treat Indian patients. Though not understanding Hindi, we saw a miracle: a lady

---

[13] Plant medicine has been illegal/controlled since early 'Church authorities preached and legislated against the practice of using plants in a magical way, for it seemed to draw on an Otherworldly power that was outside the church's jurisdiction; 'Let no one enchant herbs!' said St Elgius in AD 640. Bates, p113-114

carried her son into the room, he was unable to walk. After an adjustment, he got up and walked! There was cheering, joy, and tears, so beautiful to see.

We heard a story that Dr Naram had helped a yogi who lived in the Himalayas recover from a stomach ache. In gratitude, the yogi manifested a gold box out of thin air and gave it to him. Dr Naram had not initially believed it could be real gold until he had it checked by a jeweller who confirmed it was genuine gold.

I really benefitted from the month in India, experiencing the wonders of another culture's healing modalities and the impact of the diet, yoga, and use of intention to be healthy and happy. The only downside to Ayurveda is it requires one to stick to a limited, bland vegetarian diet and herbal prescriptions.

Tantric Lawyer Packs Mangos, Pours Drinks and goes Commercial in Northern Australia

While waiting for my next UK visa, I journeyed to the north-west corner of Australia, the small town of Kununurra and did whatever casual work I could find. I packed mangos and worked on a Sandalwood farm, with second jobs in a pizza bar and the hotel.

After three months I was tired and joined my cousin in Darwin, the northern most city of Australia, where I got work as a commercial lawyer, ran my tantric healing business, and worked Saturdays at a healing massage clinic. I was working all the time, but I didn't mind. All I could think about was moving back to the UK to continue my tantric education.

After six months of working in the Top End of Australia, I had plenty funds to return to the UK, and was very fortunate to be hosted by a friend with a sofa bed in north London. I continued the Tantra courses and my tantric healing business in Kings Cross. The healing centre advertised many kinds of therapies I'd never heard of, including "Men in Frocks, Frock Therapy for Men". I had danced with men in frocks in 5Rhythms classes, London is quite open.

Tantric Retreats at the Devon Osho Centre, 2006-2007

I attended week-long silent Tantra meditation courses in Devon at a dedicated Osho centre with beautiful gardens, a chef serving delicious, nutritious vegetarian food, a pool, sauna, and spa. One evening we did a beautiful food ritual with Indian curries and wine, feeding them to our partners while they were blindfolded. I was paired with a gorgeous man I hadn't previously met, and we connected deeply at an energetic level. Although there were perhaps ten other couples in the room, it felt as though we were alone. The ritual included our erogenous zones and was a very delicious sensation. We were in our own world of pleasure. When we came back to the room, we were amazed that some of the other couples had stopped to watch us!

The purpose of tantric ritual is not just to take you into exalted, expanded, pleasurable states of consciousness, but also to invite challenges in areas where men and women often fail to understand each other. For example, one role play we did was imagining that we were a couple settling down. The woman wanted children and a lavish lifestyle and expected the man to provide for her and their children, and the man kept wanting to retreat into his cave. Another role play was where the woman got into embodying her 'inner bitch' and then her 'inner witch' (whatever that means to the individual) and invited the man to simply observe, witness without judgement, stay present, breathe, simply encourage, and reassure her in her expression. These are examples of what we call 'embracing the shadow', embodying energies that are repressed and 'unacceptable' to express in our culture. Repression has the effect of the energies building up until they explode, often with unintended consequences.

I loved attending cross-dressing tantric parties where we got to play a character of the opposite sex. I played a bloke with a beer gut, mad about sport, desperate to get a woman into bed quickly but not knowing what to do when I got there!

I've seen, in family law, many couples separate and air their dirty laundry after staying in an unhappy situation for years. This is not the most evolved model, as it exacerbates trauma. Talking therapy helps, but may not reach the depths of the unconscious emotional landscape. Our Western laws and culture are not based on the spiritual understanding that Earth is a school and we are multi-layered, eternal souls experiencing life in a body. We have an enormous capacity for pleasure, but in the West most people are busy and stressed.

I dived deep into the tantric scene and was given practices which were "mini-relationships". You invited a person of the opposite sex to meet up with you ten times to do each practice. The meetings involved creating a sacred space, sharing, and following a structured set of exercises, sitting together in yab-yum (opposite each other or the woman on the man's lap). The exercises covered chakra breathing and massage for two to four hours!

The Bristol Tantra House – UK, 2007-2008

A group of Tantrikas invited me to live in a share-house in Bristol with them. I found the perfect place: a beautiful, large, quirky three-story Georgian manor with multiple rooms and a sunroof. Then I had to return to Australia for my visa, which took longer than expected. My visa application was refused on a technicality, and I engaged an agent to re-apply. For several months I worked a day job at a Women's Legal Centre in Australia, and at night and weekends at a massage centre by the beach. My friends moved into the house back in Bristol and very kindly and generously kept a room available for me to return to, encouraging me not to give up.

During the time I was away, sadly but not surprisingly, my young lover at the time fell in love with another woman. On my return, I threw myself into various meditation practices and seeing clients. My home practice was very successful, and I also still saw clients in Notting Hill and Kings Cross. The energy in the Tantra house was intense. One day there were four couples all doing meditation practices… sounds of pleasure and other emotions rocked the house!

The practices were about feeling sensations in our hearts and our bodies and letting go of attachment to the person, through chakra breathing (connecting energy centres) and some massage, not genital sex. My teacher used to say: "Lovers come and lovers go, only love is real". There were incredibly pleasurable and challenging times. The meditation practices evoked strong emotions such as anger, sadness, and jealousy. Feeling these, but not attaching them to the situation, we grew more self-responsible. Working with the heart continually felt like a marathon just as challenging as physical training, and with surprising results. The practices evoked joy and bliss, creating depth and intimacy between those in my community. With triggering scenarios to navigate, living in an open-relating community, we grew our maturity muscles and partook of a great experiment in how people can live, do radical tantric practices, and thrive, living together in close proximity.

The craziest tantric marathon weekend was in Cambridge with a Tantra meditation partner called Rufus. We did a four-hour meditation on the Saturday, then he took me to a gold-themed dress-up party where there was a hot tub under the full moon and ecstasy handed out freely. The two of us ended up in the hot tub kissing another couple until the early hours of the morning. Then we slept for a couple of hours and did another four-hour tantric meditation at his house the next day!

Our teachers and mentors were disciples of Osho, and the practices were extremely liberating, edgy, intimate, and confronting – they exploded myths, prejudices, addictions, and social narratives about human relating. Our teachers were protective about the meditation practices, which have been shrouded in secrecy for hundreds and thousands of years – one teacher even refused to allow us to type or email the meditation instructions!

One of the problems with tantric practices in the mainstream public domain is that they get distorted, lose their reverence and sacredness and also the joy the student experiences when hearing about a practice for the first time. Having no chance to think about it, moving straight into practice, allows the Soul and the Monad (greater consciousness connected to all of life) to experience it before the mind starts to interfere. Osho was prolific, he wrote hundreds of books which have been translated into over sixty languages. Two of my teachers had lived for years in his ashram in India. It was such an honour and a privilege to work with them and practice the teachings supported by a beautiful community.

I will share one example of such a confronting, healing practice, which I have introduced to many clients. We have an oral obsession in our Western culture due to inadequate emotional nourishment. In so-called third-world countries, mothers carry babies and children on their backs, sleep with them, and keep them close. In the five months I backpacked through South America, I never once heard a baby cry, even on a 4-hour boat trip in Lake Titicaca! The meditation is simple and beautiful, it involves a woman role-playing Mother and breast-feeding her 'child' while stroking him, giving him loving caresses and verbal reassurances. The instructions are: 20 minutes on each breast, and the woman should be well-supported with cushions and pillows. Afterwards they should not relate sexually for the rest of the day, so the man can stay in the energy and fully absorb it.

Many men are driven crazy by the desire for sex, which can be seen as a primal need to merge with the Divine Feminine, dating back to birth. And women have a need to be seen and appreciated. Other meditations were based on this desire: a woman would sit and the man just watch, both observing their feelings and desires, for 20 minutes. The gentlest version of this is where the woman is fully dressed, and the most confronting is where she is naked and the man gets to 'arrange' her body in a way that pleases him for 20 minutes!

Another pioneer of the practices we did was Wilhelm Reich, a student of Freud who developed body-oriented psychotherapy. A modern version is called Core Energetics. These techniques have been adopted into many other sacred sexuality and awakening movements. At Healing School, we had a Core Energetics teacher who came with huge cushions and bats, which we were encouraged to use to create sound as loudly and vigorously and as often as possible. I adopted a version of these release techniques into my client work, and was lucky to have spaces where this was possible.

When this need to connect with the opposite sex energy is deeply repressed, shame and guilt lock these feelings into the body. There could be an attraction for their opposite-sex parent or spouse, a desire to merge sexually with them. Or the opposite can manifest – hatred, rage, and a desire to rape or kill. When these desires are expressed and witnessed, not only verbally but physically acted out in a safe space, encouraged by a skilled facilitator, with the intention of healing, they release and create much more energy, including orgasmic energy, in the body.

Although these practices may sound weird and scary, consider for a moment the consequences of sexual and socially unacceptable desires remaining hidden in shadow: the worst is slavery of women and children, and baby factories, to feed a taste for violent child pornography – a practice some claim is more prevalent than when slavery was legal, such as makers of the 2023 movie, '*The Sound of Freedom*'.[14]

Lesson 5 – More Multiple Orgasms Please! Tantra is more than a path of ecstatic pleasure; it brings up all that is unlike Love for the purposes of healing.

---

[14] Based on a true story, the hero of the movie, Tim Ballard, gave evidence to the United States Congress, which resulted in greater cooperation with foreign countries on the campaign against sex trafficking.

Chapter 6

Dare to Dream and Do Life Differently 2002-2003

In my last year as a student at the School of Energy Healing, I got a job in a private defendant personal injury firm in central London, in exchange for more money, more hours, and more ethical dilemmas. The firm defended claims for noise-induced hearing loss and mesothelioma – asbestos-related disease – workers literally had given their lives to their jobs. There was asbestos in most buildings and no workers' compensation laws in the UK. I felt uncomfortable with aggressive defence tactics guided by financial profit targets, which distorted minds and blunted hearts. When the firm received a case of accidental death, there was great excitement as partners got hard at hitting the jackpot – it reminded me of 'The Rainmaker'.[15] I knew then – when the highlight of my week was seeing Michael Douglas and Catherine Zeta-Jones in Court,[16] it was time to take a breath of fresh air!

I Explore Breatharianism – Summer 2003 and 2005

In London I had met breatharians, people who literally chose not to eat, they lived on 'light' – and copious amounts of fruit juices, tea, thin soup, perhaps a spoon of nut butter on special

---

[15] Book by John Grisham, about corruption, legal setbacks, and victories, made into a movie starring Matt Damon, Claire Danes and Danny DeVito.
[16] Douglas v Hello! Ltd [2005] EWCA Civ 595 was a series of cases in which Michael Douglas and Catherine Zeta-Jones challenged unauthorised photos of their wedding in the English courts, resulting in OK! Magazine being awarded £1,033,156.

occasions. I never really considered '***Living on Light***'[17] as a long-term lifestyle choice as I love food, it's one of life's greatest joys. I comfort-ate through the trauma of my parents' dysfunctional separation, and we socialised a lot over delicious food with my stepdad's Jewish family. Some loved ones were concerned when I decided to embark on this radical adventure of austerity, but I never felt in any danger. I was keen to explore the benefits of emotional and physical detoxification, to experience my body a bit thinner, and to challenge habitual patterns.

The year I did my 21-day breatharian process, I also did another three months of detoxing – a month before and then later in the year, two months with a break in between. My body became so clean that I virtually stopped menstruating, did not need to use a mooncup, and had no monthly cramps whatsoever. I experienced elevated health and wellbeing in general.

I loved the three-week breatharian retreat so much that I did it again two years later at a hotel in Chang Mai, Thailand.

What did I gain from these breatharian retreats and doing life differently?

I felt an overwhelming sense of mind over matter, a lightness in my being, a certainty of knowledge that the body is so much more than the simple machine it is made out to be by Western science.

I Dream of Doing things Differently and Heal All My Relationships

Dad became interested in my healing journey, he bought the Barbara Ann Brennan books[18] we used as texts, to better

---

17 Book by Jasmuheen, who runs darkroom retreats at Tao Garden, Thailand
18 'Hands of Light' and 'Light Emerging'

understand my life choices. The books show illustrated pictures of how we can run energy, based on the five archetypes from body-oriented psychology developed by Wilhelm Reich.

One summer, after I married my second husband, Max, and planned to return to the UK, while I was waiting for my visa to be processed, I went to Byron Bay to work on an organic farm. Dad, I knew, was struggling with my non-conventional life choices. I sent him healing energy in the form of Ho'oponopono – a simple traditional Hawaiian prayer repeated to oneself: 'I'm sorry, I love you, please forgive me, thank you.' The prayer is reputed to have been used in a prison for the criminally insane, and the story is that the doctor prayed for hours over the case files of the inmates, who all recovered sufficiently that they did not need to be incarcerated. Such is the power of prayer, love and intention. Dad's traditional values clashed with mine and I could feel this, so while I was in Byron Bay, I kept doing the Ho'oponopono prayer. One day he phoned and left a lengthy, extremely loving, beautiful message – I was so grateful! I am also extremely glad that we enjoyed much quality time together before he developed dementia.

Max sponsored me to stay in the UK to be part of the tantric community we had established in Bristol. He is an amazing person, an IT environmental activist who once spent a night in police cells, wearing a polar bear suit, after being arrested at a climate camp when police claimed that camping poles were potential offensive weapons. When we met he was working on a voluntary project, a website for lending and borrowing of "stuff". The rationale was that we all have too much of it lurking in our homes. He wanted to read a book, and he was sure there were thousands of copies of the exact book in people's homes in Bristol, gathering dust on bookshelves. The Lending and Borrowing website took him months, but when he finally finished, he was extremely happy. A man wanted to borrow his expensive bike, so his principles and trust were on the line, especially when he didn't hear from the man for a few weeks. However, the grateful man returned his bike in perfect condition with a number of expensive additions. So Max's faith was justified!

Dare to Dream and Do Life Differently – Vipassana Silent Meditation, 2008

Max was happy to continue to sponsor me to stay in the UK but it didn't feel right in the end, we remained friends. After twelve years based in the UK, it was time to think about returning home to Australia. I felt like I needed a complete change, to do the opposite of Tantra, so I enrolled in a Vipassana 10-day silent meditation course. I loved the peace and stillness at the meditation centre, so I kept going back to sit and serve. Vipassana is about transcendence, silent sitting, and watching one's breath and sensations in the body, rather than getting 'lost' in them or 'becoming' the sensations and feelings. My Tantra teachers said that silent sitting in meditation plays an important, often-forgotten part in Tantra.

Vipassana meditation taught me that we are more powerful than we know. It was extraordinary how calming the practice was, and how extreme sensations in the body would arise and then subside. I kept running my tantric healing business, seeing clients in the Tantra house, and I wanted to ease my way out of it. A friend who was staying at the Tantra house was fascinated and wanted to learn what I did, so I taught her. My friend ended up taking over my business at the end of that year, and I was pleased to leave a small healing legacy to the community which had nurtured me.

At the Vipassana meditation centre, I fell in love with a gorgeous Icelandic palm reader who is still a dear friend today. We hung around together, people mistook us for sisters. I moved to the meditation centre in August 2008 to serve and deepen my practice for a few months.

While at the meditation centre, I received a distressing message from a friend that a former law client of mine was murdered by her ex-husband at a Peace Conference (and in breach of a no-contact order). Upset and disillusioned with the law, I decided to stay on at the meditation centre a bit longer. I took a break over Christmas and volunteered at an Osho retreat centre in the Canary Islands for a few weeks to get some sun. There I worked in the kitchen and taught yoga. When I returned to the meditation centre, it was covered in snow and looked so picturesque, like a postcard.

While at the centre I kept thinking of the Australian land and Aboriginal elders, it felt as though they were speaking to me, calling me home. I heard but did not take action. It was too easy to stay in a comfy rut at the meditation centre than to face going home and my conflicting feelings towards the law.

Spring 2009 UK – I injure my back, manifest healing and a new life direction on a higher soul path – my body tells me it's time to dream and dare to do life differently

Unfortunately, after a few months of too much meditation and not enough exercise, I developed a back injury – I could hardly walk! My body took matters into its own hands, and I had no choice but to leave the centre. A fellow meditator, a lovely Indian chap, gave me a lift to London. I accidentally left my phone in his car, and he invited me to lunch with his parents the next day to collect it.

After I caught a bus, hobbled very painfully to my friend's parents' place and enjoyed a scrumptious Indian meal, my friend's Dad, a retired doctor, offered to help. After some painful in-a-good-way physiotherapy adjustments, he did some traditional healing, Indian chanting, and waving of his hands. I asked why I had degeneration in my spine, and he said, "horse-riding" – which I'd not told him about. And he asked me if I missed my mother, which of course I did!

After this incredible random healing session, my back began to heal, which I encouraged through swimming, acupuncture, herbs, and massage. I knew my back would be stronger if I engaged in light exercise rather than if I took a desk lawyer job, so I got a job as an overpaid housekeeper in an English mansion for six months. I had my own generous wing of the mansion, swam in the gorgeous mosaic pool by myself every morning, and loved every minute of the country lifestyle. I looked after a cat and chickens, enjoyed fruit and vegetables from the garden, an abundance of delicious juicy berries in summer, and had meals prepared by professional cooks. The mansion was run by a kind, wealthy lady from the Guinness family whose ancestor invented the alcoholic drink. My back healed nicely, and I saved funds for my move back to Australia (via a 6-week adventure in India) to start my new life back home.

Embracing Environmentalism and the Minimalist Lifestyle – Bristol, 2010

At the Vipassana meditation centre, I had heard about people living without money. The book '*The Moneyless Man*'[19] was published in 2010 by a Bristol author, and it had a big impact on me. Later, once I returned to Australia, I would spend several years travelling, living out of a vehicle, living in meditation centres and intentional communities, and house-sitting – having a minimalist yet fantastic, varied lifestyle. As

---

[19] Living Moneyless: Mark Boyle | Moneyless.org

a Vipassana meditator and traveller, you learn that you need little more than a backpack. Even now, I still live a minimalist lifestyle, yet I still feel that I have too much 'stuff'. I could easily get rid of more than half of it, and it would not be missed.

As mentioned, I learnt that I could look the part of a lawyer through op shopping, when I lived in Darwin. I even went to the op shop on dollar discount day. At the time I worked at one of the largest commercial law firms, and the managing partner I worked with, who would fly to Sydney to buy her clothes, commented favourably on my outfits.

A Beautiful Dream of Living Differently – Permaculture Eco-Village, Christmas 2010

My interest in permaculture deepened after I moved back from living in the UK, where there are no spare inches of land. My new base became an arts eco-village an hour from a capital city, it is one of the largest (legal) community developments in the world, built to home up to about 300 people, which is the size towns used to be when people all knew each other.

Eco-design principles mean that all houses are north-facing, with high thermal mass, solar panels, rain-water tanks, ceiling fans, and insulating blinds – service bills are a lot cheaper. There is a central village wastewater treatment plant (which doesn't smell). The recycled black water goes onto the farm to water the woodlot and the extensive stone fruit orchard. There are no fences, neighbours know each other, and there is a 'help tree' to assist those who get sick, old, have accidents, or have babies. Common land is owned by all the residents, and all plants grown on common land are food-producing – nuts, fruits, vegetables or natives indigenous to the area.

At the eco-village there are always people to lend you a book or tool, give gardening help, take you to an appointment, collect you from the airport, water your garden, or look after your baby for an hour. There are regular 'gardening working bees' that always end with a cuppa and a delicious snack. Many beautiful cottage home-businesses such as cafés, pop-up restaurants, amazing food takeaways, and classes offered by residents. There are numerous interest groups that get together for bush-walking, yoga, belly-dancing, cycling, playing music, dancing, discussing books, creating art, enjoying meals, and watching movies. There are open-house gatherings, outings, and even taking holidays together. There is even an eco-cemetery where villagers can choose to be buried.

My Mum still lives in this eco-village where she is happier than I've ever seen her in my life. Surrounded by friends. An ex-schoolteacher, she gets to boss people around and tell them what to do, AND THEY LOVE HER FOR IT! She has such a good life, plenty of support, and worthy activities and projects to throw herself into. She was farm manager for ten years and is still neighbourhood group leader at the age of 80+!!

The story of how the eco-village was built is an incredible one. There is so much crazy bureaucratic red tape around housing, which assists large housing companies and governments. I think the whole 'housing dream' is a con that keeps people stuck in jobs, lifestyles, and relationships well past their use-by date. The result of following this dream is that now Australians build the largest homes in the world[20] and are more in debt than ever before.[21]

---

[20] https://www.commbank.com.au/articles/newsroom/2020/11/commsec-home-size-trends-report.html

[21] Why is Australian Household Debt High Relative to History and Other Countries? | RDP 2020-05: How Risky is Australian Household Debt? | RBA

It wasn't easy to go against mainstream trends, housing and development laws to build an alternative lifestyle eco-village. The founders spent hours, days, and weeks waiting outside government offices until the appropriate person with the power to approve the next stage or aspect of the development was available to speak with. It took incredible sheer persistence and determination from the founding directors and their core supporters, a group of artists and permaculture enthusiasts, who invested and risked their own funds and property in the venture.

Dream and Do things Differently – Return to Australia and Law

Back in Australia, I loved the atmosphere in the eco-village and enjoyed spending the summer reuniting with family and friends, meditating, and soaking up summer at the beach. It was easy to go back to law, I heard of a job, through word-of-mouth, with a lawyer I respected who ran a busy social justice firm.

I dated a polyamorous Mexican yoga teacher, Antonio, who is also a wonderful cook. I felt nourished by the relationship. We did yoga, meditation, and cycling together. We had much in common – except, with a large age difference of twenty-five years, we were at different stages in life. I set my intention for a harmonious resolution, and a few months later we parted ways, remaining good friends, getting together for meals and yoga. Years later, Antonio and his gorgeous partner looked after me after a car accident. This reinforced for me the power of love and being willing to show up authentically and do relationships differently.

I joined a Playback Theatre company, which I adored. Playback Theatre is improvisation where audience members tell their stories and watch them get played back on the spot. It isn't therapy, but it is therapeutic and fun. We were lucky to have two members who were professional actors, and a professional musician who played cello to accompany us. We were successful in gaining modest grants to perform for regional audiences and events such as Breast Cancer Awareness. There was a hilarious skit we played about a cancer survivor who lost her prosthetic breast, reported it to the police, and weeks later it turned up in a drawer at home!

Back in the world of law, I had some challenging clients: a man accused of making death threats to his wife (in Italian), which he denied. He agreed in court to an injunction (court order) not to return to the former matrimonial home. He went *straight from court to the home,* broke in through the bathroom window, and went to give his teenage son a hug. His son immediately grabbed a breadknife. The wife's lawyer called me and was so distraught I had to hold the phone away from my ear for about 20 minutes. The lawyer had a previous client who was murdered in this type of situation.

Another client, a woman, was in a bitter custody dispute over their six young children, who seemed to be with her and their father randomly in various ever-changing combinations. Whichever number of the brood she brought with her to appointments always somehow managed to destroy the client waiting area. The client and her ex used tracking apps for surveillance on each other, and there were regular incidents where one would complain of assault and other outrageous behaviour. The last straw was when the client got my personal mobile phone number (from the mobile network company) and started calling me in the evening and on weekends with constant dire 'emergencies'.

These clients needed deep healing, but there was a limit to what I could give or they could receive via the adversarial legal system. I grew tired of family law drama in general, so I set my intention for more peaceful working conditions. A friend from my meditation centre worked at a government agency and encouraged me to apply for a vacant position there with a pay rise. I ended up working in her department, with better working conditions.

I Make New Friends Who Dream and Do Life Differently

Moving back to Australia, I made new friends in the spiritual community. One tantric masseuse friend is an ex-scientist who had worked in a lab. He'd had cancer, the sort that doctors told him was fatal, he wasn't given long to live. He threw himself into healing, massage, healthy foods, exercise, anything and everything he could do to detox his system. He became a tantric therapist and got into dragon boat racing, later joining the Australian team. When I knew him, he would drive all over Australia giving tantric massages, including at ConFest (a conference/festival in the country between Melbourne and Sydney), with a signature gold tent for privacy. Women expressed their gratitude by showering him with love, donations, and various gifts. He was super fit, lean as a greyhound, and ate only pure, raw foods. He thought he could never father children but is now happily married to a younger wife, and they have a miracle baby.

Life with a Permaculture Teacher and Eco-Village Builder Who Dreams and Does Life Differently, 2012

Through the eco-village I got to know Steve, a brilliant company director of an eco-village landscape design and building company. We dated and fell in love. I shared his dream to do things differently, to live a permaculture eco-lifestyle. Later that year, I moved in with him, thus began a roller-coaster adventure…

Lesson 6 – The world is such an exciting, magical place, especially when we dare to dream and do life differently.

Chapter 7

Trust the Universe and Listen to Intuition

Wild Law Adventure – 2013-15

I attended a Wild Law conference in October 2013, hosted by a legal academic from my old university, and my world opened further. I discovered a dynamic group of people working across various disciplines to re-vision and transform law, inspired by radical thinkers Thomas Berry and Cormac Cullinan. Thomas Berry was a non-traditional priest of the passionate order, well-versed in Asian religion and philosophy, who wrote prolifically on a 'new story' for 'Earth as Sacred Community'. I was accepted into a Master's program, leaving my job a few months later to devote myself to post-graduate study and permaculture gardening, a radical and nourishing lifestyle.

I was in love with the Wild Law movement (or Earth Laws as it was later renamed), which fuses politics, legal theory, quantum physics, ancient indigenous and Asian spiritual wisdom into a new vision for humanity. The international movement to recognise rights for Nature and the Universal Declaration of the Rights of Mother Earth were proclaimed in 2010. Wild Law presents a vision of how systems could transform to support a viable role for humans within the Earth community. For me it was a ray of light in the barrage of depressing evidence connecting law and governance to the promotion of the disastrous exploitation and destruction of Earth. Wild/Earth Law is both an activist and academic movement to re-vision society, a manifesto for promoting social and environmental justice, the conservation of biological and cultural diversity, animal rights and welfare, and green spirituality. Dismantling and transforming these systems is necessary to ensure that the pursuit of human wellbeing enhances the beauty, health, and diversity of Earth instead of diminishing it.

I discovered things about our legal history, like that the Australian Constitution was reputedly written in a week by a few white aristocrats on a boat trip with cartons of cigars and whisky. Australia still does not have a treaty with Aboriginal and Torres Strait Island people, although Victoria now has a Treaty Act, and most Australian Governments have promised funding for treaty negotiations. In Australia nothing in the natural environment has an inherent right to exist, unlike in New Zealand and many other countries such as India and Brazil, in which legal rights for rivers and parks are recognised.[22]

The Native Title Act 1993 in Australia, which recognises Aboriginal connection to land, was a political compromise led by former Prime Minister Paul Keating, who went against his own Labor Party colleagues to make a deal with Aboriginal elders. Prior to this law, Aboriginal people's connection to their land was not recognised. The Native Title Act is a minefield of constantly shifting legal technicalities which no lawyer who doesn't specialise in the area can hope to decipher, an uneasy truce with mining, pastoralist, private and government interests.

Aboriginal Elders, Permaculture Magicians, and Environmental Activists Trust the Universe and Listen to Intuition

We were at the centre of this new crowd, environmental and indigenous activists, and life was busy and very social. I

---

[22] Legal personhood for nature has legal ramifications – Lane Neave

felt privileged to do regular voluntary work with a dynamic, formidable Aboriginal Elder, the late Georgina Williams, then a Senior Kaurna woman. Georgina's ancestors came to her spirit fire and told her to build a cultural centre for her mob (Aboriginal community group). On a voluntary basis I assisted with the organisation of Georgina's vast library representing decades of activism and was often drawn in to help with her latest political cause. Steve and I were involved in Aboriginal cultural projects at the eco-village with master's building students from Canada. We hosted students at our home, and enjoyed Aboriginal educational cultural tours. I learnt a lot about the ancient culture, still visible just beneath the trappings of the city. For example, Aboriginal people had healing knowledge through herb lore and used bark to splint broken bones.

I feel so grateful to have seen the incredible wide-open spaces, waterfalls, rock pools, and glorious, mysterious Aboriginal artwork, which varies considerably in style, the earliest reputed to have been of sky beings. I was tuned into the grief and pain of Aboriginal peoples and the Ancestor spirits, through voluntary work with Georgina. I also saw the happy results of activism in wetlands saved from developers. Through Steve I met many gentle permaculture magicians like our late kind elderly neighbour whose chickens ran into part of our garden. We would help her with heavier pruning and mulching tasks, and we often came home to find gifts of fresh produce, eggs… her tomatoes were prolific and tasted so good.

It was a lovely lifestyle – the amazing Garden of Eden that Steve designed and that we worked in together became my office. I set up a portable desk under the pergola, so I could move with the sun. If the weather was too hot or cold, I sat at the dining room table overlooking the magnificent garden. My desk was next to the fish pond with water lilies, flowers and vegetables, the huge banana palm, red juicy dragon fruit, white sapotes… It truly was a real-life Tropical Paradise. Steve was a member of the Rare Fruit Society, we had delicious produce all year round. With our wide circle of friends, people were always popping in, and we hosted numerous parties and dinners. When we travelled, we had so many people to stay with, and we often had people stay with us for short or longer periods of time.

The only snag was that the happier I was in my study and work, the more the relationship between Steve and me deteriorated. He reminded me of my stepdad, they were both brilliant visionaries, pioneers of alternative lifestyles, independent thinkers, and forces of nature. Steve triggered me in a way reminiscent of my stepdad. I felt shame and embarrassment as I left and returned several times, trying everything to make the relationship work, to no avail.

To make matters worse, the law firm I consulted in part-time was sold. My PhD in Earth laws, which had been the bright-light driving force of my life, hit a brick wall. My supervisor, a former radical, gained university tenure (permanent employment) and pulled in his activist horns. My thesis got bogged down in the theory of Earth jurisprudence, how to apply it, whether to apply it to existing law or Critical Legal Theory, or Critical Race Theory, or Critical Race Legal Theory – and yep there are far too many 'criticals' here… !

The last straw was a bitter family court trial I was instructing solicitor on. On the day of the trial, the star witness, my client's mother, took an overdose of painkillers, staggered off to a Church across the road, and refused to return when she was due to give evidence. The barrister I instructed to appear for my client teased me about 'standing up for the rights of vegetables', as we drank red wine at the end of each long day in court while we debriefed.

Steve and I went our separate ways. He was desperate to return to the bush.

Listening to Intuition on an Outback Roadtrip and Rediscovering Tantra – Spring – Summer 2016-17

A few months later I took off on my own on a roadtrip for five months to re-ignite my passion. I did a delicious yoni women's course, volunteered at an Osho ashram in Byron Bay, volunteered at meditation centres, and gardened on remote rural properties. This trip led me to retrain in tantric journey work overseas, and when I returned, I launched my second tantric healing business at a beautiful house on a quiet tree-lined street rented by a dear friend, Mike, who teaches Alexander Technique. Mike stayed at the cottage half the week, and the other half with his partner, so it was available to use the rest of the week. Mike and I met through Vipassana meditation and Playback Theatre. We both have a passion for healing, spirituality, and meditation, so it worked to share the house in this way.

I had so many beautiful, inspiring clients, and it was such an honour and privilege to again be offering this work in the world.

When I wasn't seeing tantric healing clients, I worked in law part-time. For a few months, I worked in-house assisting an Italian family building company who were in a David and Goliath federal court battle with a multi-national to resolve their dispute. I helped build their legal precedents. After that work was complete, I worked part-time for a Filipino law firm, which was colourful and varied.

I also travelled to a Tantric Taoist ruined city called Hue in Vietnam on an eco-tourism university study trip and learnt a lot about the extent of the Taoist empire throughout Asia – I admired the feng shui of the beautifully designed, impressive buildings and gardens.

LESSON 7 – Trust the Universe, Listen to Intuition – WHEN ONE DOOR CLOSES, ANOTHER OPENS.

Chapter 8

You are More Powerful than You Know

I found that when I moved back to Australia, my weather magic did not work, I couldn't connect with the land in the same way. Maybe it's because I know Australia is one of the driest continents and needs more rain, at least the majority of the country does. Aboriginal people have always done weather magic, but the rituals are traditionally complex and lengthy. I have had to surrender the weather magic piece.

There was one notable exception. A small group of us did a very special outdoor mushroom ceremony at Moore River in Western Australia, and we sent the land and Aboriginal ancestors healing. The place was an Aboriginal mission, made famous in the movie, '*Rabbit-Proof Fence*', based on a true story about three Aboriginal girls who escaped from the Moore River Native Settlement, north of Perth, to return to their homes 1,500km from the Australian rabbit-proof fence, while being hunted by police and Aboriginal trackers on horseback.

On the evening of our ceremony, the weather forecast was for fine, sunny weather. We had enjoyed a day on the land, walking and swimming in the river. During the ceremony, the weather changed, there was thunder, lightning, and rain. Luckily it was light, as we were camping. It was as if the weather had joined in cleansing and healing the land of the scars from the past trauma carried by the First Nations descendants and in fact all of us.

The weather healing experiences really taught me that there is a greater plan to the Universe, higher powers at work way beyond the ability of the rational mind to perceive. We are more powerful than we know. Other power revelations came through Mystery School initiations.

Mystery School Temple Training – New Zealand, 2018

One of the most challenging things I have ever done is a six-week temple training at a Mystery School in New Zealand. At an International School of Temple Arts (ISTA) course in Sydney, I heard about the Mystery School in New Zealand. I enrolled at fairly short notice and found when I arrived that there were actually four tantric lawyers in our group, and one academic, which seemed quite high for a group of twenty-four. I explored particular initiations on power and love at Mystery School, which all showed me how free we can be.

Mystery School Love and Power Initiation 1 – Go towards Eros

It was an open-relating community, we were encouraged to go towards attractions to run eros with people we liked.

There was a gorgeous man, Tom, I was attracted to, he was in my first pod (small groups that met daily after brekkie for a check-in). He confided in the group that there was someone he was attracted to, and I just knew it was me. When Tom was near, my stomach did flip flops and my body had tingles. Yet I hung back from exploring the connection as he was the husband of my teacher, Marie, whom I liked and respected. I felt very shy. A facilitator gave me a nudge to explore our love connection, so I surrendered to it and it was beautiful.

Tom and I ended up sharing a room for the last two weeks of the course and had a very wonderful time together. The big challenge and awkwardness came once Marie arrived at the Mystery School. I was in the moment and the flow with the connection, and realistic not to have any expectations for the relationship to continue outside the Mystery School. To allow oneself to deepen into love and intimacy, following energy in the moment without planning, is both challenging and incredibly beautiful.

Since this love affair I have chosen to remain celibate, to focus on self-love, balance my inner feminine and masculine, my personality, Soul, and connection to all of life. I feel extremely grateful to have a wide circle of friends, including many gorgeous men and women to enjoy fun and activities with. I also feel like I've had perhaps more intimacy than most people have over several lifetimes!

I have so much respect and gratitude for the Mystery School and ISTA – they are massively popular and provide a brilliant service to the world. They have also been through a huge journey around tightening up their rules and boundaries and handling feedback and complaints, which I have been happy to assist with when asked.

Mystery School Love and Power Initiation 2 – Go towards triggers and aversions with Eros

There was an American man, Braveheart, who triggered me greatly. I found myself cringing when he was near and even avoided him.

A couple of weeks into the course, the facilitators suggested that we lean into and go towards our triggers or aversions as well as our attractions with eros, which was revolutionary for me. I decided to lean into the invitation with Braveheart. Once we ran eros together, conscious connected breath, I discovered a well of compassion towards him, and the aversion disappeared. We even spent a beautiful night together in the forest temple with an open fire.

Braveheart was a Shibari master. Shibari is the Japanese art of tying someone up in erotic and artistic ways, and a friend in my pod suggested that I try it – it's fantastic for getting out of the mind and letting go of control. We can't truly experience the ecstasy and mystery of the universe while we are hanging tightly onto the reins.

I asked Braveheart to do a Shibari ritual with me, and we found a place in the huge garden beside the roses – it was so transformational and liberating to be tied up, and it was also incredibly erotic! I learnt at the Mystery School what an extraordinary amount of different forms of love it is possible to feel.

Mystery School Initiation 3 Love and Power: Use Your Skills to Grow Where You're Planted

When I went to mystery school, I was working solely as a tantric healing therapist, having a break from law, which was satisfying, but my brain felt like it was getting lazy. After the temple training, Marie suggested that I not reject my legal and academic skills.

I learnt how to do clearing using muscle testing, called 'The Spiral',[23] which I added to my tantric healing client sessions. I got a job in the law in a country town and flew back to the city once a fortnight to see the tantric healing clients – which was wonderful and exhausting.

---

[23] Clear Your Shit, Dane Tomas

Empowering Youth to be More Powerful than They Realise

I strongly believe that a version of the ISTA exercises should be taught in schools to all children on the planet since employing the tools would lead to a much healthier, happier world – it could eliminate sexual abuse, rape, domestic violence, unwanted pregnancy, traumatic break-ups, covert affairs, and family court litigation – the unconscious cycle of multi-generational PTSD that is handed down by our ancestors and pervades our world.

The ideal sexual consent conversation is extensive, including not only preferred contraceptive use but also current and past sexual history, sexual health, sexual preferences, desires, and boundaries, as well as preferable post-sex care required. Without agreement on all these things, the sex is likely to be under par at best or traumatising at worst – leading to unwanted penetration, pregnancy, or Sexually Transmitted Disease.

ISTA teaches the Wheel of Consent developed by sexologist Betty Martin, exercises where participants explore different forms of consent: taking, allowing, serving (giving), and accepting. The motto is: if it's not a 'fuck yes' in your body, it's a no. [24]

New Age Festival People Power

When people get together for a common purpose, they are more powerful than they know. There is a true story that happened at a Burning Man festival in America a few years ago, attended by about 20,000 people. A woman was raped, the offender fled and hid, was searched for by a vigilante crowd and was eventually found, as there was nowhere to hide. There was a

---

[24] https://bettymartin.org/category/wheel-of-consent/

hugely emotional confrontation with no physical violence – the offender was racked with shame, guilt, and regret, he apologised profusely to the woman. The crowd woke him up to who he was: a good man at heart but full of pain, a man who made a wrong choice and was capable of redemption and change.

First Nations Lore Empowers

A positive culture can exert much power on anti-social behaviour. If an Aboriginal child developed destructive anti-social tendencies, they had to stay at camp with their Elders rather than go on hunting and gathering expeditions. If that child continued in their destructive anti-social tendencies over a long period of time, which was extremely rare, that person was excluded from the Tribe, as a last resort. In African tribes, if a person was hurtful or destructive, their loved ones stood in a circle and called that person's name, **CALLING THEM BACK TO WHO THEY REALLY ARE**.

Aboriginal law and lore in Australia is possibly 125K years old and is encoded in Songlines, stories, chants, and poetry about plants, animals, and seasons, by which First Nations people can navigate lands they have never visited and find food, water, and shelter. There can be 100 verses for one plant. In Africa, ancient ironworks thousands of years old are known about due to songlines that are based on a woman's sexuality.

The Story of My Teacher's Teacher's Teacher of Taoist Healing in a Cave in Remote China

There are many stories of spiritual teachers exerting extraordinary powers. A teacher of Taoist healing I worked with in northern Thailand, Dr Mantak Chia (author of '*The Multi-Orgasmic Man*'), told an interesting story about his teacher who came from China.

The teacher had heard about monks who lived in caves in the remote mountains in China, and he wanted to find them. He knew roughly where they were, but the journey took so many days he kept running out of food and water and having to turn around before he got there. He managed to find some local people who helped him find water and food in the jungle environment, and he was able to carry on with his quest.

It took him many years from embarking on his journey until he finally arrived at the caves in the mountains. When he arrived, the cave was in very poor condition, animals had made it their home, it seemed unfit for human habitation. And his worst fear was realised: there was a body in the cave covered in caked dust and dirt for many months or years. His heart fell – the better part of a lifetime's quest wasted, he thought, he was too late and had failed. He turned to leave and go home with a heavy heart.

Then, he heard a cough. A miracle – the body was alive! The man who would become his teacher sat up, looked at him, and said: "Good, you're finally here. Your first duty is to wash my body and clean this cave. Then we can begin!"

The teacher was out of his body, journeying in the astral planes (non-physical realms of existence) until his disciple arrived. He was able to put his body in stasis, a state of balance or equilibrium, where his organs had virtually shut down but not completely, his body was able to survive without food or water.

A True Story of a Powerful Ancestor

My Mum's cousin Deidre tells the powerful story of her mother, Great Auntie Daisy, who taught herself to be very physically strong and fearless. She grew up in a remote dry inland farming place and loved to ride her horse long distances to the beach and back, and in storms, which took hours or even days.

When she came of age, she decided to ride her horse to the city to seek her fortune. The voyage took days, she encountered a fierce storm and very strong wind. She lay down with her horse to wait out the storm, covering herself in a blanket for the night. When the storm passed she didn't give up, she kept on going.

In the city she gained work in a domestic position (the common option for women at that time). One night she was walking through the city and realised she was being followed by a man. She turned down a street with shops and their doorways slightly off the footpath and hid. The footsteps kept on coming. She knew that the assailant had seen her hiding place. He kept coming to face her. He started to grope her, undid his trousers, and took out his member. Aunty Daisy gave it a Chinese burn with her strong forearms, and the man fainted!

She stepped over his body and made her way home.

When asked by her daughter, was she scared, she replied confidently, "No, I was just waiting for my moment!"

Lesson 8 – You are so much more powerful than you know!

Chapter 9

Slavery to Sovereignty – The Hidden Gift in Covid-19 – Know Thyself

Covid-19 ended the job I had with a Native Title organisation I had only been at a short time, as access to Aboriginal communities was stopped, and I returned to my home state. I threw myself into fitness, going on long walks and gardening, and did a three-week detox retreat. I set up my own online legal and mentoring business; people could not come for in-person tantric sessions. Working online from home has given us so much freedom, having more options is more relaxing. I recall the first Tantra festival I attended online, I was amazed at how I could feel energetically connected and turned on despite the distance!

Although I initially struggled with technology and working online in my business, I ended up being very successful. I know now that my Soul recalls past life echoes from ancient civilisations, like Atlantis and Lemuria, where there were devastating wars due to unethical use of technology, and gene technology experiments. I also feel resonance with Aboriginal, indigenous or First Nations people, who care for land rather than own property, and who choose to evolve without technology and with very strong, rich spiritual lives. We can only try now to live in balance with nature. I still choose not to own property, I trust my ability to manifest what I need in terms of homes and income.

Down the Rabbit-Hole of the Coaching Cult in Search of the Freedom to Work Online

During COVID-19, I ended up spending over $100k on high-end coaches and ended up in spiritual cults. Looking back, my behaviour was like any other addiction, like drinking, gambling, or drugs – it started light-hearted and was fun, controllable. The investments began small. I'd temporarily silenced my own inner voice due to the 'rules' of the cult, which were to submit to the coach. In hindsight I feel that it was an extremely valuable learning experience, it taught me a lot about power and sales. Moving in these circles, I saw what is possible in terms of online business, and I was able to attract more complex interesting legal commercial work. I learnt to push through and stay with the resistance to finding and sharing my voice – the first time I launched a group challenge, I was actually physically ill – my coach saw my superpower to help women decide whether to separate and to give them a powerful divorce.

I had encouragement and support to develop another way, a better way, of attracting and working with clients with legal and emotional problems. As I'd noticed, unfortunately, the legal system has a way of retraumatising people due to its adversarial nature. The mentoring work I did not only solved their legal issues, it also healed much of the emotional angst caused by the stressful situation. More on this in the next chapter!

Sometimes you learn more from life not working out as you think it should, as life puts you where you actually need to be.

To V or Not to V

I moved to my father's home city during Covid-19 in order to bond with him in his golden years, and with other family, but that was difficult since he felt vulnerable and chose to isolate. I had to have a job before I arrived, the State border restrictions were such that had I remained self-employed, I would not have been granted entry. Courts were bringing in rules that allowed for telephone hearings, and legal practitioners were not permitted to attend courts unless they showed proof of vaccination. I am so grateful that I was never in the position that I had to decline a client's case, court hearing, or job for not being vaccinated. I haven't done licensed drugs for decades and I've been perfectly healthy, so why would I start now? It is very ironic that for a short time I worked at a law firm and drafted numerous mandatory employer vaccination policies.

I went into therapy for a while, focused on the love connection Dad and I shared. Dad's final parting gift to me is to spare me the pain and discomfort of witnessing his decline. I'm so grateful that in the last years before dementia, he has made the effort to visit me several times. Twice he came alone and we spent several days together. He was able to attend my 50th birthday and made a speech, telling my friends and family how proud he was of me and how I helped grow my parents up!

Unfortunately to V or not to V has been divisive – and as someone who rarely uses pharma products (except vitamins) and has had no vaccinations for the past thirty years, I struggle to understand the controversy. The more drugs and vaccinations we take, the less our bodies naturally produce those substances.

I disagree with legislated or mandatory vaccinations of any kind – the government were careful to say it wasn't mandatory, yet the advertising campaign and restrictions on so many activities and going to public places certainly felt like a breach of human rights.

I have been asked numerous times what people's legal rights are when they are dismissed for declining a COVID-19 vaccination. I had a client I represented for an Unfair Dismissal Application. She had actually had COVID-19 and received an exemption from her doctor when she was dismissed. I drafted several pages of extensive grounds of why the dismissal was harsh, unjust, and unreasonable. Our case relied on, amongst other things, the Nuremberg Code 1931, Article 5:

'Innovative therapy may be carried out only after the subject or his legal representative has unambiguously consented to the procedure in the light of relevant information provided in advance. Where consent is refused, innovative therapy may be initiated only if it constitutes an urgent procedure to preserve life or prevent serious damage to health and prior consent could not be obtained under the circumstances.'

This is a clear statement of principle on the right to choose one's medical treatment. Yet I was informed by the Tribunal that they had no jurisdiction to hear our case, and that if we proceeded with it, we would lose and get a costs order against us, which would mean that my client would have to pay all of her former employer's legal costs. We therefore had no choice but to withdraw.

It's unfortunate that vast billions of dollars have created slick advertising campaigns that brainwash people. The four-part British television documentary, '*The Century of the Self* explains in detail how advertisers teamed up with psychoanalysts to sell products through fear and guilt.[25]

The Power of Our Intention – We Are Divine Manifestors, Let's Manifest Sovereignty!

I have been working for the last year on a project I've dreamt about and prayed for – it's been wonderful to do interesting

---

[25] 'The Century of the Self', a 2002 Series directed by Adam Curtis tells the story of mass-consumer growth

work that aims to make a difference. We all have these heart-and-soul projects, dreams, and desires, no two are alike, and no one can find it for you. You need to go into the dark, the unknown, the Void… and allow the unexpected to happen! It is part of our birthright as humans to manifest our reality through the power of our intention.

My personal heart project was Ancient Lore meets Western Law, developing a new, cutting-edge law providing much-needed recognition for Aboriginal Traditional Knowledge. It was my dream job, working with government and stakeholders to rectify wrongs, re-writing His-story. Social justice is something that has been a motivating factor in finding my 'Big Why' since my teenage years.

Sovereignty, Truth, and Healing

I observe many Australians fearful and uncomfortable of "truth-telling", facing our collective past in relation to the origins of our modern society, the thorny relationship with descendants of the First Australians. I understand from both my healing and law work that telling the truth with compassion and non-judgement has a great deal of power. It means that anything is possible. If people don't speak honestly about the past, their trauma – if they cannot confront the truth, healing and connection possibilities are limited.

Life is short, and in my experience the best, RICHEST, MORE REWARDING path is the one less travelled, expressing and living truth and aliveness through the heart and soul.

Knowing Thyself as Sovereign – Not Healing the Past is Slavery

After a year on this project, I'm moving into my spiritual Soul work fulltime. There is significant tension between recognition of Aboriginal law, Indigenous Cultural Intellectual Property Rights and anything which could potentially pose a threat to the status quo. Yet there's been a purity and a beauty in coming together to feel as though we are making a positive difference, trying to establish better systems and processes which are more enlightened, fairer, and take into account past injustices.

As a psychic healer who grew up supporting my parents, I can tune into and *become* what the client or external work environment expects and needs of me. As I grow more conscious, I am self-responsible for my choices and feelings, and I see all environments I'm attracted to as places to learn, play, and grow. I also see our life choices as karmic, in that we are attracted to environments and people that assist us in our process to open our hearts.

I have such a familiarity with and connection to law, lore, records, and processes – over hundreds of lifetimes, perhaps thousands, which to me explains why I am writing this book, to show that there are far better, more enlightened ways to be, to live, to thrive and to resolve disputes. This is where law and lore are very different, one is based on truth and love, the other is based on an outdated cultural narrative that serves the agenda of a global elite minority.

I feel that to heal our karma, which can mean remembering our past lives, overcoming any blocks is true freedom. To remain stuck in karmic loops of victim mentality and behaviour is slavery.

Two Forms of Law – One based on Slavery, the other on Sovereignty

There are two forms of law on the planet: Spiritual law embedded in Tantra and the Tao, which is combined with Earth-based indigenous law on the one hand, and Western law on the other. Spiritual law and Earth-based First Nations Laws are based on a Duty of Care to others and the Land – maintaining harmony with each other and their environment.

In First Nations communities there were no jails, no old folks' homes, no dementia, and no hospitals. Life wasn't perfect, and it's easy for a Tantrika like me to fantasise about group orgies all day and night long – haha (which probably rarely happened, if ever, by the way, but it's SUPER FUN to imagine!)

The conduct of modern corporations was analysed in the 2003 documentary film, *The Corporation*[26], and deemed to be psychopathic – words used to describe a pathological liar, impulsive, with lack of empathy and superficial charm, a history of shady conduct, and a riddle of contradictions. The film featured interviews with Noam Chomsky, Michael Moore, and others. Western Governments cannot rule without financially successful mega-corporations, who all but dictate what to write in our laws and how to enforce them.

The tech explosion is like *The Sorcerer's Apprentice*, the cautionary tale in a delightful Disney movie *Fantasia*, yet most people are unaware that the human body is the most incredible machine already – it can produce whatever substances we want and need, on-demand, it's chock full of healing power.

However, it's so awesome that more folks, especially in the post-COVID-19 era, are community-minded – running home businesses online, seeing complementary health practitioners, creating intentional communities, establishing temples and eco-villages, running festivals, local produce markets, and barter or gift economies – practices more akin to what communities have done for thousands of years. We can truly make our own rules

---

[26] *The Corporation*, a documentary film by Mark Achbar, Jennifer Abbott, and Joel Bakan.

now about how and where we want to live – this is something which was previously only available to the elite in society.

Lesson 9 – The healing journey takes us from slavery to sovereignty as it inspires us to follow our own intuition, trust, take responsibility, and believe in miracles as though they are usual.

Chapter 10

Your Unique Soul Path

There are so many life lessons, healing modalities, practitioners, and teachers that have contributed to my healing journey. Part of my aim in writing this book is to share my experiences for you, the reader, to inspire and motivate you to let go of fear, invoke the courage to follow you heartfelt dreams.

Inspirational Stories of Change and Growth

The purpose of this chapter is to illustrate that the amount and extent of change that's possible is unlimited – what I've seen over the years has really blown me away and inspired me no end.

I experienced a lot of sudden, radical, challenging change in my life, particularly as a young child, and eventually learnt to embrace change, making it work for me. I became, in effect, a catalyst. Change just happens around me! I have an uncanny knack for connecting people, a talent for seeing the possibility and potential in people and situations, trajectories of events. This relates to my healing training to increase intuition and Akashic record readings, the journey of our Soul.

Our Spiritual Tribe

Just as my teacher's teacher sought out his teacher in the remote caves of China, and I sought out my teacher of Taoist healing in northern Thailand, took his courses, bought his books, learnt the practices, and passed them onto clients – so you too, dear reader, have a spiritual tribe.

It used to be the case that spiritual teachers required their students to devote themselves 150% to their teacher, to follow their suggestions, directions, and practices precisely. Many spiritual teachers, lineages, and practices still require this. Vipassana meditation, most forms of Yoga and Qigong, and Taoist healing are three examples. This rigidly disciplined approach never really worked for me.

I feel it is important for me to respect and listen to my clients, whether in law or healing, and to offer my guidance as a suggestion to be taken on only if it feels right. What I love about healing and mentoring work is the opportunity and ability to encourage the personal growth of others. It is indeed truly an honour, a gift, and a privilege to witness and support others when they are at emotionally vulnerable places. To help others become stronger, more resilient, is truly empowering.

The Unique Soul Path of Change

Change can occur anywhere, including in the most unlikely places. For example, a law client of mine, who was imprisoned for a long time for a serious criminal offence, changed his life remarkably. He found a book called '*We're All Doing Time: A Guide to Getting Free*',[27] and he worked at the practices, taking up meditation, yoga, and a clean diet like a duck to water. He became, in short, a model prisoner and human being. When he told me about the book, I was in my late twenties, still quite new to spirituality, and I'd just had my second bike accident. I got a copy of the book and used it for the easy yoga practices, illustrated by cute cartoon yogis. It helped me in my recovery, and I recommended it to many people.

---

[27] 'We're All Doing Time: A Guide to Getting Free' by Bo Lozoff (Foreword by the Dalai Lama)

Early Inspirations – Witnessing Radical Positive Life Changes

1. My first partner Gus, who is extremely bright, left his boring–as-batshit job as a shop refitter for a supermarket chain, and despite leaving school at fifteen, he became a teacher. I had faith he would succeed. He enjoyed a beautiful, fulfilling career until he retired.
2. Gus's mother Rose, (another bright spark) never finished school but went to uni in retirement, got a masters in English literature and wrote several books. She is still writing and publishing into her late eighties.
3. My first legal secretary, Sue, had a lot of potential. She was from a terrible background and lacked confidence. I encouraged her to follow her passions. She became secretary to the Director of Legal Services, made Italian pasta with her partner, trained in environmental health, runs marathons, owns a beautiful home with a vegetable garden, and works as an environmental health officer for a regional council.

Radical change requires support and commitment to the inner work.

When I was teaching at the School of Energy Healing and working as a healer, I supported clients with all kinds of issues, including 'difficult' diseases such as chronic fatigue.

The Miracles I am Not Allowed to Speak About Due to the Law

I supported a student, Roz, who was journeying with cancer. During her time at the School of Energy Healing, Roz managed to become cancer-free – however you are never cancer-free according to the authorities, you go into remission. At this point it is necessary to add that it is against the law for anyone to say that they are able to cure cancer. It is probably obvious to you, the reader, at this point, that I am an advocate of questioning medical diagnoses, taking responsibility for your health, and coming to your own decision regarding your medical treatment.

Cancer is an extremely emotive disease. I have lost a number of dear relatives to cancer: my uncle, my stepdad, his ex-wife, and his partner's daughter. It is not legally allowed to advertise that any clients have healed themselves of cancer.

The Cancer Laws date back to the post-war period when people with cancer were treated with the first chemotherapy drugs that were developed from the chemicals originally used to make mustard gas. The First Cancer Act was passed in the UK in order to lend money to the National Radium Trust – a forerunner of modern radiotherapy treatments. The law also stipulates a blanket ban on advertising cancer treatments to the general public. Modern Cancer Acts provide that anyone in breach can be fined or imprisoned for up to three months.

I do not wish to take a dogmatic position on any particular kind of treatment; I am simply making the point that this is an example of the vast resources spent by governments, and the net result is that:

1. People become very fearful of a disease.
2. They are funnelled into an 'interventionalist' treatment regime.
3. No one is allowed to say they can assist in curing the disease using alternative methods
4. The mainstream 'interventionalist' treatment regime is then seen as mandatory and also as the most effective.

5. The law is based on giving 100% power over to the 'authorities' and does not acknowledge the inherent healing power of the body.
6. The law does not acknowledge healing modalities from other cultural traditions, such as Ayurveda, Traditional Chinese Medicine, and Traditional Aboriginal Knowledge of Healing – which probably makes it racially discriminating.

To me the Cancer Laws are inconsistent with the sovereignty of the human body, our rights to make choices about our bodies. I feel it's really important not to get hung up on judgement about what the law says or doesn't say, other than to remind you, the reader, that we create our own reality. The most amazing healing journeys I have had myself, and supported clients on, have been ones where there has been 100% responsibility taken.

The suggestion in my story is that YOU are in charge of your life and your body – and it is so important that we remember this. It's interesting in this context to examine our OWN ideas and beliefs towards authority figures and our bodies. And my SUGGESTION is to take back the power we previously gave them, or at least to hold that lightly as an OPINION based on the best they know given that person's background and training.

What does "CURE" mean?

The word CURE is very interesting. It comes from the medieval Latin *curatus,* "one responsible for the care (of souls)", past participle of *curare* "to take care of".

It also meant "care, heed, concern, trouble" – with many more extensions over time it also means "of healing, successful remedial treatment of a disease", from the old English "ward off, prevent, defend."[28]

My invitation is for you to TAKE BACK YOUR POWER – to consider that YOU, my dear reader, are in charge of your precious Soul.

The best possible results I have seen in the hundreds or even thousands of clients I've helped came about when clients consult others and then trust their OWN instincts. I'm an unusual practitioner in that I can see and commune with your Soul, with permission, I really see not only its beauty and perfection, but also where it seems kind of squished, compressed, or bored in your life, and where it would just LOVE to have fuller expression.

Sometimes this fuller expression can look kind of messy, at least at first while the pipes are cleared.

Energy Follows Thought

Have you considered what happens in your body if I say, "Don't think of sucking on a lemon"?

What happens? Your mind can't help but picture a lemon and imagine the taste in your mouth.
There is a reason I rarely visit doctors unless I have an accident or need a certificate, or to check a diagnosis – that reason is that they are Dis-EASE focused.

IT IS MY CHOICE TO **FOCUS ON UNLIMITED HEALTH, EASE AND FLOW.**

---

[28] https://www.etymonline.com/word/cure;

My experience is that healing in my life, whether it's a broken heart or a broken limb – works best when I do the following:

1. FEEL FIRST. Take a walk, a run, bath, sit quietly on your meditation cushion, dance, go into the bush or to the beach or to a mountain, to wherever you feel relaxed and spacious.
2. BREATHE INTO THE SENSATION. I invite you to be curious and to expand your inhalation to your belly – energy follows thought.
3. ALLOW SOUND to come with your breath. Sigh, shout 'Ahh' or whatever words want to be spoken or shouted or whispered.
4. MOVE YOUR BODY as it wants to move, shake your hips to some music.
5. INVOKE YOUR INTENTION. Here are a few of my favourites:
   I wish to be healed of this situation, what can I learn from it?
   I am powerful, I deserve abundance, ease and flow.
   How is this situation in my best interests?
6. GIVE GRATITUTE GRACIOUSLY. I have often had a practice of listing, journalling the things I'm most grateful for in my life – my relationships, my money – allowing myself to feel safe, loved, and abundant.
7. DEEPEN INTO YOUR DESIRES, DREAM BIG. These can be varied, expansive and changable. Mine: was birthing a cutting-edge new law for Aboriginal traditional knowledge recognition and protection, and family healing, now launching a new international spiritual business, and living vibrantly to 102 when I will leave my body consciously.

This works best when you are completely honest – let go of judgement and allow yourself to go deep into the situation and ask, what is it you really want to experience?

Be open to receiving guidance here. We often get what we need at a soul level rather than what we want!

HOW I TURN PAIN INTO POWER

I look at the most painful situations of my life and how I gained something, what I learnt from them.

My examples:

1. I lost my Dad when I was young and gained a Stepdad who gave me experience of other cultural traditions, taught me I am the most powerful person in my reality, and encouraged me to think independently.

2. My parents were at war my entire childhood, in Court and on the doorstep when my mother pulled one of my arms and my father pulled the other. I ran away into the garden as they were both acting crazy. I chose not to go with either of them. This taught me that people generally ALWAYS act crazy when they are going through a painful separation.

3. I allowed feeling down, depressed, even crazy, (which passes) when I was in the process of separating from Steve, the brilliant but then troubled permaculture eco-village builder. I had helped him resolve his chronic sore neck, referring him to a physiotherapist friend. I helped with easing his depression due to legal company issues by spending weeks going through years of his emails and paperwork, and referred him to a mediator I knew. At mediation, they not only resolved the dispute amicably, but THEY HUGGED and cried together. I helped him 'find his mojo' again, accompanying him on his dream holiday to go on a 4-wheel-drive trip of Western Australia – he prospected for gold, I walked and read about Earth Laws. After two or three years,

I felt so angry and resentful because I had prioritised Steve's goals and ignored mine for years – I had fallen into an old female pattern in society. I decided to write a court claim, an affidavit, about it, and I sent it to a barrister friend. Her advice was short and sweet: "Don't do it." I'm so glad I followed this – Steve and I resolved our issues and stayed friends. Because I understand this 'crazy', having been there myself, I love to support clients to navigate disentangling from partners, homes, jobs, and businesses that no longer support them when they desire to leave.

I HAVE TURNED MY WOUNDS INTO SUPERPOWERS. I CAN HELP YOU TO DO THE SAME.

CLIENT MIRACLES I CAN TELL YOU ABOUT:

With my one-on-one clients, we start a session chatting over likes and dislikes, expectations, desires, intentions, boundaries, and edges. I do muscle testing to ensure the energy is as high as possible, clearing any negative emotions.

Activation of energy is next, I ask and can often see or sense where clients are holding their energy in their body, I encourage the client to let go with the breath. In the breathwork and bodywork, there is a clearing of blocks, an opening of energy.

In the last session I gave, my client an anaesthetist kept feeling energy in his hands, saying he had never experienced so much in his body and hands before.

After I set up my second tantric healing website based in Australia, I attracted clients from a range of backgrounds. I saw a number of high-achieving corporate clients who were especially dedicated to their health and healing process, they made time for regular sessions.

Tantric Healing Client #1

A corporate client came to see me because his steady partner wanted to get married, but he wasn't a 100% fuck yes. He loved her dearly and couldn't imagine not living with her, so he couldn't understand why he felt the way he did.

He confided that he had had sexual experiences with a male classmate as a teenager and occasional homosexual fantasies since then. After working with me over a period of six months and exploring his feelings, he and his partner decided to open their relationship and bring a man in. They had a steady relationship as a threesome, and sometimes there would be twosomes, this is what worked for them. I encouraged him to have honest and open communication and to express and take responsibility for his feelings, desires, and needs. He reported back a year later that they were still extremely happy in their stable threesome.

Tantric Healing Client #2

I saw a lady who came for two-hour sessions once a fortnight over three months. Her main issue was that she felt in a rut in terms of her life generally. She wanted to share her special, creative healing gifts but felt stuck.

Through our work together, she became more in touch with her body, emotions, and desires. She realised that she had given too much of her power away to her family and her boyfriend, who were very important to her. She gave herself permission to start sharing her gifts, planning and actioning a long-held dream to travel to the UK. After we finished working together, she finally took the bucket-list holiday of her dreams and had a wonderful time.

Sexual Issues:

I have worked with many male clients in my tantric healing business who suffered from what is labelled erectile dysfunction, the inability or difficulty to get erections, and premature ejaculation, ejaculating earlier than is desired. This is much more common than you might think. When men are growing up, self-pleasure is often furtive, fast, and furious – there can be shame or guilt around sexual desires which feel strong and overwhelming – and a need to 'finish' quickly before the parents or siblings interrupt.

During COVID-19, I started to combine law and mentoring online, here are four people I helped using my unique skill-set:

Mentoring Client 1

My client, a young woman from America, reached out as she was in the process of making a compensation claim and felt it was difficult to deal with, she was postponing. She had fulfilling work, a partner and young children. She had been sexually abused by her gym coach as a child and had to make a statement in support of her claim.
We worked on clearing her emotional blocks using muscle testing, and we discussed her statement – she sent it to me and I gave her feedback. The blocks related to suppressed emotions from the past. Once the blocks had been cleared, she was able to proceed with her claim.

Mentoring Client 2

My client, a separated Mum from Hawaii, reached out as her ex-partner, the father of her child, was giving her problems. She wanted to stop him having contact with their son, and thought the only option for her was to report his behaviour to police and take out a restraining order against him. This would have been quite costly for her to do privately through a lawyer. We discussed the behaviour of her ex that was unacceptable, and I encouraged her to write a clear letter setting out boundaries and conditions on which she was prepared to allow him to see their son. I made some changes to the letter, so it was still written in her voice (not lawyer-speak), but it was also firm, non-judgemental language, and I deleted anything that was inflammatory, unnecessary, or accusatory. We also cleared some negative emotions she had towards her ex and the situation.

She reported happily a few days later that her ex had agreed with her conditions, and she was very pleased that she avoided the extreme action of legal proceedings and a restraining order.

Mentoring Client 3
This client, contacted me as she wanted to leave her husband, whom she loved platonically as a dear friend. She had felt for a decade that she no longer wished to be married to him. She held a lot of fears around how she would survive financially and cope emotionally on her own. She also worried about how their teenage child with special needs would cope. She told me from our first meeting that without support she didn't think she could find the strength or courage to leave. She was deeply in love with another man but had resigned herself to not being able to experience that togetherness due to her feelings of guilt and obligation to her husband and child.

We worked together for three months, one session every fortnight. We did muscle-testing, clearing negative emotions – fears and doubts that came up for her around separation. We worked through all her fears and also her practical needs one by one. We addressed them one at a time, and step by step, together we made a plan that I supported her in implementing.

Although separation and independence were out of her comfort zone, nothing went as badly as she feared. She was able to find and move into her own place around the corner, so her child could easily go between houses. She experienced so much joy in setting up and decorating her beautiful new home. Her self-worth increased as we worked on increasing her prices and being open to receiving from additional sources. She saw herself in a different light and applied for jobs that she wouldn't otherwise have. As I write this, I recall that I have just seen a drop-dead gorgeous photo of her on social media, advertising her new brand, website, podcast, and delicious offerings – she looks and sounds incredible, magnetic, magical, alluring, funny, attractive...

I am soooo proud of her and our work together!

I feel truly blessed to have opportunities to use both my healing and legal skills to assist women through separation.

Mentoring Client 4
Penny got in touch with me to support her in separating from her husband and to help her come to fair settlements for property and child support. With three young children, she was feeling terrified and overwhelmed at how she would cope as a single mother. She also felt very angry and let down by her husband because there was no longer passion or intimacy in the marriage.
However Penny's husband was unwilling to work through these feelings with her. Penny and I worked together to clear her emotions – the anger, sadness, disappointment,

guilt, shame, and fear of leaving her husband. Together we kept visualising her new life where she would be free to enjoy her independence and pursue her desires. We reached an amicable win-win agreement, which was unusual in that she received both a lump sum and high weekly child support, which put her mind at rest in starting her new life. I drafted the Court agreement that was used in the settlement, and we also had a separate Binding Financial Agreement for child support registered with the Child Support Agency.

Reaching these amicable agreements required these steps:

1. Clearing emotions and setting intentions
2. Client gets assertive, asks business accountant for past business statements and financial returns
3. Establish the matrimonial asset pool
4. Client gets more clued up about money
5. Consider how to divide the asset pool
6. Clearing more emotions
7. Re-setting intentions for an amicable, powerful separation
8. Negotiation from a powerful place, setting up a win-win intention for settlement
9. Bringing it home: putting the house on the market, getting the agreements done and dusted.

From the hundreds of clients I've represented, worked with, and seen in court, I strongly feel that **THE PROBLEM TODAY IS PEOPLE DON'T KNOW HOW POWERFUL THEY ARE.**

The solution, what people need to know, is:

Proven steps to activate their power and set them free to create the life of their dreams.

But what to do when you have literally tried everything?
…I hear you ask.

I believe it's the Universe's way of saying try another way. When one door closes, another always opens…

It's an opportunity, time to look at things, at yourself, at life itself… another way!
Challenges are a Signpost to our Highest Soul Path, they help us to lean in and find our courage!

Find Your Meaning and Purpose in Life – Be Your Best Self

"Each person comes into this world with a specific destiny – something to fulfil, some message has to be delivered, some work has to be completed. You are not here accidentally–you are here meaningfully. There is a purpose behind you. The whole intends to do something through you." – Osho

Earth is a school – a bit like a playground or video game, and it's important to understand the rules in order to know how to play. We often forget that we, as a collective, make up the rules and create what we believe.

For most people, consciousness often operates on auto-pilot – we are like the fish who are swimming and can't see the water we are in. These are the unconscious or barely conscious thoughts and feelings that sweep through our bodies.

I believe that our Soul chooses its lessons, parents, and soul contracts with others, knowing what we are in for before incarnation.

Part of the fun of the game is the amnesia – our learnings from other lives are wiped from our memory before we incarnate.

Exploring consciousness on other planets and on Earth at other times is very different to what we experience here and now. I can recall being a ball of light and creating what I desire with my thoughts instantaneously. Equally, I can recall misusing my power and using my thoughts to cause harm to others.

The rule of manifestation on Earth at this time is as follows:

1. We have to match our vibration with that which is desired.
2. There is a time lag.
3. The Soul chooses its experiences and lessons.
4. Life is most fun and harmonious when we can match our conscious desires with our Soul urges.
5. To really enjoy playing the game, it's best to get to know your Soul – and if you don't know what I mean, find a mentor, a guide, a friend, or do practices to connect. I have included a selection of books, references, and practices at the end of the book to help you.

Listening to intuition helps to navigate change, deal with even huge losses, and make the most of opportunities.

Sometimes life brings grief and disappointment. When people leave or we lose things in the material world, it makes us draw more upon our inner resources – what doesn't kill us truly does make us stronger. If we allow it to, we become like a multi-faceted diamond, shaped and smoothed until we sparkle all over.

Here are three examples of following the rules of manifesting dreams while following intuition:

1. **Match your vibration with that which you seek.**

    I believe it's important to be equally comfortable enjoying a beer at a working-class tavern and taking tea with the Queen of England at Buckingham Palace.

I have learnt to match my vibration with clients while working in many areas of law in Australia and London, and working as an energy healer, tantric healer, and online mentor with a huge variety of people, from those who are chronically ill and on welfare benefits to multi-millionaires, high-flying business people, lawyers, doctors, and sports professionals across five Australian States (Perth, Adelaide, Melbourne, Sydney, and Darwin), in London (Notting Hill and Kings Cross), Bristol, Bath, Tao Garden Resort in Thailand, and Reykjavik in Iceland.

2. **Look for opportunities:**

   There were plenty times I was scared or unsure where to go next, but I kept putting one foot in front of the other.

   In my life I have manifested a huge variety of experiences, life-changing adventurous travels, and relationships with remarkable individuals and communities.

3. **Know you are a powerful creator – when you ask the Universe with your heart and Soul for something, and then let go of the result – you can bend space and time, people and events will move around you.**

   I have so many examples from my life and those of my clients when this has occurred. The catch is we often just want more 'goodies' (experiences we deem positive or beneficial, more cash, property, better health for ourselves and our loved ones) – this is normal; however, in my experience, the price of spiritual initiation also means making space for the new, letting go of what no longer serves us.

Being somewhat accident-prone in my younger years and trusting that there was a higher purpose, taught me to look for the silver lining and follow the current of life wherever it took me.

If I'd had a "normal" upbringing (whatever that is) and received everything I needed on a platter growing up, I wouldn't have become an independent thinker, able to remain healthy and fit at 55 years old, without using any pharma products except vitamins for the past three decades. But for the trauma, I wouldn't have sought therapy, and I don't think I would have become devoted to service to others, which is a constant discipline and incredibly rewarding.

Akashic Records – the Journey of the Soul

From the ancient ruins on Earth, my own past life memories, and what I've read and learnt, it's obvious to me that those of us who are old souls have been through a great deal, and our conscious minds are protecting us from the traumatic memories.

When I work with clients, I ask permission to open their Akashic Records, the journey of their Soul. I receive impressions, mind pictures, colours, feelings, sensations, I hear and smell things. This is my extra-sensory perception, which I have trained myself to use, and it is within everyone's power to do this too. These impressions from the Soul records give me symbols, messages, images – which speak directly to the Soul and help navigate the next steps for optimum growth.

My Vision for the Future – A Blueprint for Future Society

Humans are naturally intuitive and loving – these beautiful qualities can be enhanced, so we live truly in tune with nature and other inhabitants of the planet. The Japanese scientist Emoto has shown, through beautiful water crystal pictures, the importance of our energy – how it made a vastly different design when he printed and placed words like love and peace beside the water and played classical music, versus playing death metal music and displaying words like hate beside the crystals. This is the human potential – to master our energy and experience systems, processes, and institutions that foster and encourage self-responsibility, consciousness, creativity, and ecstasy.

Being coached and mentored throughout my life has made such a difference for me to be the best person I can be. Friends have inspired me with fitness, and professional coaches with what's possible in the business world. I would love to see communities coming together, shifting into eco-villages designed around passions and interests, like-minded folk supporting each other. I've stayed in numerous communities where this is the norm rather than the exception. Instead of current events programs and newspapers being focused on the lowest common denominator of the human experience: violence, war, corruption, and scandals, they could broadcast what is possible at the opposite end of the spectrum: stories of love and hope, caring for each other and our land.

Clearing Blocks and Quantum-leaping to the Highest Possible Vision for the Future

It is a sunny, cool Saturday in early winter. I do a park run as usual and head to an all-day workshop. A handful of people from different backgrounds are at the workshop to meet our past and the best version of our future selves.

I want to let go of the fear, grief, and anger from what triggers me – my father's dementia, our estrangement, all the various injustices in the world and in my past. And I want to invoke forgiveness, courage, strength, and power. I've been drawn recently to pick up a book by Dr Brian Weiss, a psychiatrist who has specialised in past-life regression therapy for several decades. I am calling in understanding of what I've learnt in past lives and pulling this wisdom through to the present.

The first meditation: connect with our mother, the maternal line, feminine ancestors

I see my mother and my two grandmothers looking at me, beaming with love, and my heart explodes with joy. Then the scene changes and I'm a gypsy, wearing heels and dancing wildly to music played by a group of musicians. I'm totally into the dance, feeling the ecstatic current, wild and free, and I'm aware that people are watching me dance. Then the scene changes again, and I'm a Priestess of Avalon, dressed in a blue homespun robe and cloak, a blue spiral is painted on my forehead, and I carry a staff with a spherical globe crystal at one end. I'm enjoying the sacredness of the ritual and the camaraderie with my sister priestesses.

The second meditation: connect with our father, the paternal line, masculine ancestors

First I see my Dad and then my stepdad, who I lived with from the age of eight and who passed away over twenty years ago. I haven't thought about him so much lately. I see how much time we have spent together, living in the same home for twelve years, the ups and downs, all the efforts we both made to understand each other.

I see my last meeting with my stepdad before he died of pancreatic cancer in April 2002. I see how I knew it would be the last time I would see him, I felt sad. I sat on his lap, so our hearts were together, and I hugged him. We stayed like that for a while, and I felt so much love and gratitude – I had forgotten about that. I did energy healing on him and sent love to his pancreas. He was amazed and told me how proud of me he was, and that I had gone places he could not have imagined. I felt extremely privileged and grateful to have known the love of two very different fathers, and I felt my heart truly receive and absorb all the precious gifts of their time and love.

In the third meditation, we meet our past life self

I was a Greek queen, Goddess Athena, it was a matriarchal society. I wore regal dress, gold jewellery, flowing feminine robes showing off a bit of skin. It was warm and balmy. I was very happy. My whole life felt like a moving prayer, very sacred. I saw myself riding horses, eating at banquets. And I didn't have a husband to fetter my freedom, I had a small harem of men who were very close friends and lovers, I recognise four from this life (Gus, Steve, Adam, and Matty).

Then my life changes, there are armies invading, led by religious men. They are dressed in black, call us heathens, and are very scathing of our lifestyle. They condemn our Gods, desecrate our sacred temples, destroy our statues and books, everything we hold most dear. It is truly terrible how invading armies not only seize power and destroy lives, but also destroy everything so they can control the people. I escape safely through tunnels, but I have to leave my two daughters (younger half-sisters in this life). I am grieving the loss, it cuts me like a knife wound. I can hardly breathe, but it is the only way I can keep them safe. The only way I survive is by cloaking my identity, changing my name, hiding who I am – my true nature, my beliefs, and values – and pretending to adopt the patriarchal, materialistic culture of the invaders, a culture that worships a punishing God. I can never reveal who I really am to anyone. I appear to be compliant but inwardly I am seething, and there is a part of me which will not submit. It seeks revenge!

Quantum Leaping into the Highest Timeline with the Most Potential

In the final meditation, I see myself trying to learn more about indigenous lore, but it feels like chasing rabbits down burrows, a bit like a wild goose chase. This was one of the things that I wrote I wanted to manifest, but it doesn't exactly pan out in the future self I tap into.

I see myself instead running workshops and being deep into Mystery School esoteric teachings. This is a big part of my life now, I am doing a nine-month Teachings of the Temple online course, meditating daily, connecting to Earth kundalini and the black hole at the centre of the galaxy, spending time riding the event horizon.

My Future Self tells me to Follow My Bliss

I see myself dressed in colourful clothes of natural textures, in a warm climate, walking barefoot in the bush with others, laughing and singing, gathering mushrooms and herbs in baskets. I can also see myself at the Mystery School in New Zealand. I'm running workshops in abundance, detoxing, yoni mapping, and g-spot and ejaculation mastery. I'm also working online, charging $2-5k for client sessions. The most I have charged until now is $1,750 for a recent one-to-one half-day tantric session, so it's quite a jump but apparently my future self has already done it.

I see myself having made peace with my parents and spending the last six months of my Mum's life with her. We write a book together, about her life, called Ray of Light, which is appropriate since her name is Rae, and when I was born, she sang the song 'a little ray of sunshine has come into my life'.

Spiritual Guidance for Embracing Power and Wisdom Through the Heart:

I believe that the vast majority of people are not living their full potential, .

On a recent plant medicine journey, I was connected to the Cosmos and the Black Hole at the centre of the Milky Way Galaxy, and I kept seeing fractals, the Fibonacci sequence. I also saw and felt myself as various animals, including an elephant at a time when they were considered sacred in India. It was so funny having a trunk! The elephant represents majesty, wisdom, longevity and a link to ancestral wisdom.

The elephant is also related to my current stage of life, 'the Crone'. The word is of Gaelic origin, and Celtic traditions are rich with mythology about a divine older woman:

'The Crone, *Cailleach*, [or 'veiled one'] has universal qualities: she is not a goddess of fertility of death or of any one thing but is a deity who is both transcendent and immanent. She is connected with rivers, lakes, wells, marshes, the sea and storms; with rocks, mountains, boulders, megalithic temples and standing stones.'[29]

I am past the female change of life, since Steve and I decided not to have children a decade ago. At that time, I spoke to my menstrual cycle, thanked Her and told Her that as She was no longer required, she could leave. And so she did. For aeons, women have connected with their bodies in this way – there are ancient Taoist meditations specifically for this purpose called 'Slaying the Red Dragon'. The advantages are that as the body is no longer producing eggs, this conserves precious life force female energy which in the Tao is called 'jing'.

---

[29] Crones, Excerpt from **Secret History of Witches**, © Max Dashu 2000 (www.suppressedhistories.net)

Since then, I have had sporadic brief visits from the Red Goddess, such as when intensely practicing a lot of tantra five years ago, and more recently when younger female relatives with children were bleeding. In the last five years I've not been guided to physically take a lover, though I'm blessed to have beautiful loving heart-felt soul connections with members of both sexes and enjoy regular bodywork.

The plant medicine journeys and other signs showed me it's time for me to leave the project on Aboriginal traditional knowledge to which I'd given everything I had and devote myself 100% to my spiritual practices and business, in order to fulfil my destiny. I was given valuable guidance about only expressing a fraction of my potential, that on some key relationships, and dark feelings of not fitting in, which have plagued me my whole life. Personal and planetary ascension requires the Tantric Lawyer to come fully out of her witches broom closet, to be seen and heard, to dance around the fire, laugh a mad cackle and sing the song of her soul frequency with all her heart! I'd been fantasising for years about moving to Bali, and finally the time has come for me to act – a new life beckons... The world needs the visionary magic and embodied Earth wisdom I have been blessed to have experienced and embodied - it has been my complete honour and pleasure to share my story,

Blessed Be Dearest One, never doubt how beloved you are by the Universe, or underestimate your true power and potential.

Thank you for reading this, from the bottom of my heart to yours! 😊

If you enjoyed this book, please connect with me at: <u>http://www.thetantriclawyer.com/</u> and receive your free gift

Ways to Join my Community

- *Free Facebook Group:*
  **https://www.facebook.com/groups/106073525203
  1541**

- *LinkedIn:*
  **https://www.linkedin.com/in/kim-the-tantric-lawyer-
  582b2413/?originalSubdomain=au**

- *Subscribe to my YouTube channel:*
  **https://www.youtube.com/channel/
  UC8vjko54dtOlmvRESQdtesQ**

- *Email:* **thetantriclawyer@gmail.com**

Meet Your Highest Future Self – A Ritual

It is sometimes said that when we do our own inner healing work, it helps seven generations backwards and forwards to heal.

I'd like to invite you to consider for a moment the lives, stories, and legacy of your ancestors.

Bring to mind a picture of your parents, and of your grandparents, and your great-grandparents.

If you have any photos or sacred objects from them, you can make an ancestral altar.

Consider for a moment, what were their lives like? What sort of work did they do?

Did they work the land, have a craft, make clothes, grow food, raise children, keep animals?

How do you think they felt about life? What were their core beliefs?

Which countries (and in what circumstances) did they come from originally?

What sorts of activities did they do for recreation? Did they like reading, music, dancing?

Were they religious, and if so, what sort of role did religion play in their life?

What were their underlying beliefs and values around subjects like the land, animals, spirituality, God, education, money, work, food, family, sexuality, the body, and community?

Consider how their strength of character and passions manifested in the world.

How are you similar to them and how are you different in your feelings, choices, lifestyle, values, and preferences?

Know and honour their intention to make a better life for their children.

Let go of any limiting beliefs that no longer serve you.

Allow yourself to feel and absorb the gratitude for the gifts they gave to you in your genetic lineage.

Give thanks and close the ritual.

Acknowledgements

This book would not have been possible without the support of many.

My deep heartfelt gratitude to Dave Thompson, Davina Davidson and Keziah Daniel from Inspirational Book Writers. Thank-you for nurturing the vision of this book from its early stages to completion, for providing grounded and encouraging feedback throughout, and for creating a beautiful nourishing community – I couldn't have asked for better support! 😊

Thank-you to my kind generous friends who read manuscript samples, showered me with moral support and wrote enthusiastic testimonials, Sarah Phoenixfire for the Preface and Kate McIntyre for the Foreword.

Useful Resources

HEALING, MANIFESTATION, EMBODIMENT

5 Rhythms Dance: (https://www.5rhythms.com; *check your country/area)*

The Abundance Book, John Randolph Price

You Can Heal Your Life, Louise Hay

The Body is the Barometer of the Soul, Annette Noontil

The Secret Language of Your Body, Inna Segal

Clear Your Shit, Dane Tomas

Hands of Light *and* Light Emerging, Barbara Ann Brennan

Becoming Supernatural, Jo Dispenza (Book and YouTube meditations)

We're All Doing Time: A Guide to Getting Free, Bo Lozoff

The Hidden Messages in Water, Masaru Emoto

Endeavour College Australia (runs discounted student sessions)

Dr Gabor Maté (Books and YouTube channel)

Vipassana meditation

TANTRA

Emotional Detox Through Bodywork, Mal Weeraratne

The Multi-Orgasmic Man, Master Mantak Chia

Osho

Ma Ananda Sarita

Margot Anand

David Deida

DIVINE LAW, EARTH LAWS and WILD LAW

Thomas Berry

Australian Earth Laws Alliance

Songlines: The Power and Promise, Margo Neale & Lynne Kelly

Listening to Country: A Journey to the Heart of What it Means to Belong, Ros Moriarty

Aboriginal Peoples, Colonialism and International Law: Raw Law, Irene Watson

First Knowledges' Law: The Way of the Ancestors, Marcia Langton

True Tracks, Respecting Indigenous Knowledge and Culture, Terri Jaenke

Wild Law, Cormac Cullinan; Wild Law – In Practice, Maloney and Burdon

Should Trees Have Standing? Toward Legal Rights for Natural Objects, Christopher Stone

Changing the Rules of the Game, P. Higgins

SACRED ECONOMICS

Small Is Beautiful: A Study of Economics as if People Mattered, E.F. Schumacher

Sacred Economics, Eistenstein

The Spirit Level, Wilkinson and Pickett

SPIRITUAL and DEVOTIONAL

Autobiography of a Yogi, Paramahansa Yogananda

Anna, Grandmother of Jesus, Claire Heartsong

Poetry of Miriam Rose, William Blake, Rumi

Music of Deva Primal and Miten, Fia, Parqois, Wendy Rule

DETOXING

Living on Light, Jasmuheen

Cleanse and Purify Thyself, Richard Anderson

The Cure for All Diseases, With Many Case Histories, Dr Hulda Clarke

TAROT ORACLE CARDS

Goddess, Lemuria, Earth Magic, Osho, Isis, Star Seed Oracle

REVISED HISTORY

Fingerprints of the Gods, Graham Hancock

The Chalice and the Blade, Riane Eisler

The Real Middle Earth: A History of the Dark Ages that Inspired Tolkein, Brian Bates

My Name:

My first name 'Kim' means 'record keeper'.

'Mukti Nirjhara', my second and last names are the spiritual names I was given by Sarita, one of my Tantra teachers in the UK – Mukti means liberation, freedom, Nirjhara means waterfall.

Notes

121

Notes

122

Notes

Notes

Notes

Notes

Notes

Notes